CW00522215

THE INSIDE STORY OF THE LITTLE TEAM THAT TOOK ON THE GIANTS OF F1

For Jane & Alby

First published in March 2008 by Veloce Publishing Limited, 33 Trinity Street, Dorchester DT1 1TT, England. Fax 01305 268864/e-mail info@veloce.co.uk/web www.veloce.co.uk or www.velocebooks.com.
ISBN: 978-1-84584-160-7/UPC: 6-36847-04160-1

Readers with ideas for automotive books, or books on other transport or related hobby subjects, are invited to write to the editorial director of Veloce Publishing at the above address.
British Library Cataloguing in Publication Data - A catalogue record for this book is available from the British Library. Typesetting, design and page make-up all by Veloce Publishing Ltd on Apple Mac.
Printed in India by Replika Press.

FORZA MINARDI!

THE INSIDE STORY OF THE LITTLE TEAM THAT TOOK ON THE GIANTS OF F1

Contents

Foreword

You have to try pretty hard to spend 21 seasons in Formula 1 and not once get on the podium.* But if you're going to do something badly, at least do it in style. Even with the open goal that was Indianapolis 2005, Minardi missed. How could anyone love such a bunch of losers? Well, tens of thousands of F1 fans did love Minardi and the reasons are slightly more layered than they may first appear. The cars from Faenza weren't always a mobile chicane. In fact, they were rarely 'blue flag merchants' at the back.

The Minardi roller coaster involved many dips and precious few highs but, at its best, the little Italian outfit hit the front row of the grid and even led a lap. For many years, it punched way above its weight and, of course, it was the nursery for future stars, including the youngest ever world champion, Fernando Alonso.

Under-funded from the very start, Minardi somehow outlived far more illustrious names like Tyrrell and Lotus. When the going got really tough in the new millennium, when Prost and Arrows went to the wall, Minardi staggered on. In the final years, the highlights were points in Melbourne and Indianapolis. But in 2005 the game was up – the remaining privateers could no longer keep their heads above water and Minardi was sold to an international conglomerate.

Unashamedly, this writer is biased; I love Minardi. If that makes you frown, I hope this book will win you over. If you already understand, enjoy the memories.

A wise man once said scoring a point for Minardi was like 'Dalla stalla alle stelle' – going from the stables to the stars. You have to know the bad times to appreciate the good. God knows, there were enough bad …

(* Full marks if you remember Mark Webber and Paul Stoddart on the Melbourne podium in 2002, but the celebrations were for a fifth place and unofficial.)

Acknowledgements

I'm lucky; incredibly lucky. I've 'raced' Nigel Mansell in go-karts and laughed out loud as that famous red, white and blue helmet lapped me. I've been driven around Fiorano in an F430 Ferrari sports car with Michael Schumacher as my chauffeur. I've interviewed Lewis Hamilton before he was famous. But nothing gave me as much joy as watching Minardi stick one over the big boys. Ralf Schumacher sailed past me as he crashed out of the 2002 Australian Grand Prix, and little did I know it would be the prologue to one of Minardi's finest hours. I was sitting next to an Italian Ferrari fan who was initially bewildered by my support for Minardi. As the race reached its climax, he too found himself cheering for Mark Webber, almost forgetting Schumi had won the race. We embraced as Mark crossed the line and I don't mind admitting my vision was impaired by some moisture.

Its hard to rationalise support for The Other Italian Team but three years later, as Minardi F1 was consigned to the history books, it struck me if anyone was going to write the 'history book', it may as well be a journalist who had a soft spot for the team. I hope you find this a balanced yet affectionate account of what went on, as told by the people on the inside. From F1 to A1, GP2 to F1x2, Champ Cars to Le Mans, the Minardi diaspora is cast far and wide. I thank everyone who has helped me for their time and effort and I salute every single member of staff at Faenza who worked so hard to achieve so much against such great odds.

Gian Carlo Minardi and Paul Stoddart are the first to heap praise on the small army of staff, but they were the generals. I thank them and wish them all the best for today and tomorrow.

I must also thank Christijan Albers, Fernando Alonso, Luca Badoer, Eddie Baker, Gianmaria Bruni, Adrian Campos, John Castleman, Antonio Cazzago, Aldo Costa, Anthony Davidson, Lisa Davis, Bernie Ecclestone, Giancarlo Fisichella, Christian Fittipaldi, Victor Fuster, Rodrigo Gallego, Luis Garcia, Marc Gene, Glen Gibson, James Gilbride, Matt Goodwin, Damon Hill, Rodolfo

Intelisano, Tony Jardine, Graham Jones, Ted Kravitz, Roberta Leonardi, Bradley Lord, Jaime Manca-Graziadei, Nigel Mansell, Eddie Marrian, Pier Luigi Martini, Sir Stirling Moss, Alessandro Nannini, Fernando Paiva, Regine Rettner, Luis Perez Sala, Richard Salisbury, Terry Stuart, Jasmina Verstraeten, Murray Walker, Ron Walker, Mark Webber, Justin Wilson, Alex Yoong and Enrico Zanarini.

Its fair to say I'd banged on a few doors before I found a publisher with some vision in Rod Grainger at Veloce. I am grateful to him and his team for all their support and guidance and also to Damien Smith at *Autosport* magazine for renewing my enthusiasm. Also of that parish, Nigel Roebuck and Mark Hughes, Bira Goren at *Autosport Atlas* and, at *Motor Sport* magazine, Rob Widdows and Martin Nott.

The *Grand Prix Data Book* is an absolute gold mine for all motor racing fans and essential in researching a book such as this. Thanks to David Hayhoe for his special appendix of Minardi statistics here.

Good photographs are so important in books like this. Thank you to all the unnamed snappers who often take greater risks than we realise. Also to Giorgio Nada, Nicola Storey at Sutton Motorsport Images, and to Robert Murphy and Dennis Vogel in the USA.

Which came first, the book or the website? The answer is forzaminardi.com, and I thank its founder Robert-Jan Bartunek for agreeing to the use of this great salutation in the title of my book. RJ has been a constant support and I thoroughly recommend his website to those who appreciate the finer things in motorsport. Emmett Quigley of Minardi Club San Francisco has also galvanised and advised me, and he does excellent work spreading the word. It has been great fun to meet the faithful at Grands Prix in Italy, Spain, the UK, France, Austria and Australia. I wish I had a photo of the happy German camper at Magny-Cours who'd bedecked his entire caravan with pictorial tributes to Minardi. Naturally, his bemused friends were all dressed in Schumi red.

My journalistic colleague from Sicily, Salvatore Toscano, has been invaluable in his efforts. His English is much better than my Italian but I can say 'mille grazie' to Salvo. For his advice on the wonderful world of publishing, I am very grateful to Jonathan Lloyd at Curtis Brown. This project would never have happened without one James Hunt fan turbo-charging my enthusiasm back in the late 1970s; thanks Dad.

I couldn't have put this together without the kindness of strangers, all brought together by the family that is Minardi. All anecdotes and information have been supplied in good faith with the caveat that, of course, any mistakes here are my own.

To all these people and to the others who helped, not least my wife Elizabeth, my profound gratitude.

Simon Vigar
London

What was the point?

Two Fridays separated by 20 years. "It was a Friday morning, the 5th of April, 1985," says Gian Carlo Minardi. "For everyone in this sport the main goal is to run in Formula 1. We managed to get there and it was a beautiful day."

Fast forward to the rather ugly night of Friday March 4th, 2005. "I was too tired to think straight," says Paul Stoddart. "God, I'd love to live through that moment again because I agreed to back off. With hindsight, I wouldn't have and the history of Formula 1 would be different today."

Some ask 'what went wrong?' The real question is 'what went right?' How on earth did a bunch of chancers survive for so long? The team never had much money and then, in the last two seasons, it had a boss on an apparent kamikaze mission. Ironically, the modest business model which ensured Minardi's survival as an independent constructor was soon obsolete. Yes, it allowed the team to 'tick over' for ages but it was the sound of a dying engine. The team based in a timber yard in rural England was already proving this and Tyrrell had a far greater pedigree than Minardi. 'Speculate to accumulate' was not in the DNA of Gian Carlo Minardi, a flaw identified by some of his most loyal lieutenants. 'Motorsport' had become, in the words of Sir Stirling Moss, 'motor business'.

So what was the point of Minardi? Well, here's one. "It was difficult, very difficult," says Fernando Alonso. "I came from winning in the previous category. To get used to seeing yourself in the last positions was very frustrating but it was one year to learn, one year to get experience, and I convince myself not to not stress me out too much."

Of course, it did him the world of good. Many Minardi graduates, Fernando included, say it was the perfect way to announce themselves in F1. No-one expects the car to do well so any movement up the grid, any chance of getting in the points, people will sit up and take notice.

The first thing you realise when talking to people about Minardi is the smile. These are battle-hardened Grand Prix racers yet the smile is not one of pity nor sarcasm, it is one of genuine warmth. People like talking about Minardi because most people are romantics, most people like backing the plucky underdog. Much of the Minardi secret was team spirit, which you can't buy, no matter how rich you are. If Minardi was everyone's 'second favourite team', that affection was magnified by its Italian-ness. It was a 'family team' where people stayed for years. Some of the original staff from the early eighties remained in the Toro Rosso era. Minardi welcomed others in the paddock with beautiful pasta and coffee; the canteen a haven for Ayrton Senna, among others. It was also trying to succeed in the shadow of a much bigger team just up the road. Enzo Ferrari and his acolytes have always ensured Italian competition has been suffocated, albeit with a smile, and Minardi probably snuggled up too close for its own good.

For the racing purist, there is as much merit in spotting a small team fighting epic battles as there is appreciating a dominant season by Ferrari, Williams, McLaren or Renault. For the masses, Mansell-mania, Schumi's 'Dekra-heads' and Alonso's Spanish army are as inevitable as they are transient. Yet glory chasers can have a rather unpleasant edge, especially when you're sitting next to them in a grandstand.

Bernie Ecclestone is often characterised to be at the other end of the F1 scale to Minardi; unsentimental, big business, Darwinian. But the F1 ringmaster misses Minardi. And he has a sense of humour too; if you are put on hold as you wait to speak to him you hear, on a loop, the Stealers Wheel song made infamous in the film *Reservoir Dogs*, "Clowns to the left of me, jokers to the right, here I am, stuck in the middle with you."

"It was part of Formula 1 growing into what it is today," says Ecclestone on the demise of Minardi. "Gian Carlo played an important part and although he was always at the back of the grid you need to have someone there. He was no trouble and did whatever he could to help Formula 1. They shouldn't have had success considering the sort of planning they had behind them."

Minardi had success in the late eighties and early nineties but it is in the record books for the wrong reasons. 52 races before scoring a point will take some beating. How about most Grands Prix without a pole position? One of its stalwart drivers has the record for the most 'pointless' races. Minardi is second only to Arrows in the table of most GPs without a win.

Overall, it doesn't look good – so what was the point? Well, there were some wonderful moments, a period of genuinely great expectations, and it was a business too. Gian Carlo Minardi put an ordinary Italian town on the map, hired locally, and got to indulge his passion for motorsport. In the latter years, Minardi served a purpose for 'the show' as a whole. It was a place for the big teams to try out young drivers (Trulli, Alonso and Webber) and it made up the numbers. As Bernie says, someone has to be at the back and more than one of the big teams was relieved to still have Minardi there. It's no coincidence that, post-Minardi, the Honda-backed Super Aguri team was rushed onto the grid for 2006 in much the same way as Paul Stoddart's Minardi five years earlier. Aguri was using even older cars, purchased from one P Stoddart.

As big money changed the economics of F1 forever, all three remaining privateer teams sold up in 2005. Of Sauber, Jordan and Minardi, the Italians had lasted longest in the piranha club. If that isn't some sort of success story, what is?

Apprenticeship

Enzo Ferrari hated smoke, but how was Gian Carlo to know? Anyway, there was an ashtray on the table …

"I smoked a full packet while talking with him. He didn't say a word. Later, I was reproached by Sante Ghedini, Ferrari's assistant. There was this marvelous yellow ashtray with Ferrari's trademark in the middle. I remember it vividly. I was quite nervous. I just kept talking and smoking for three, four hours. Ferrari at his desk was lit by three spotlights, so you can imagine the amount of visible smoke when Ghedini entered that room."

The smokescreen couldn't hide Minardi's passion and Enzo Ferrari agreed to supply him with some of his precious Formula 1 machinery. Minardi were, in effect, the last Maranello privateers, except the team wasn't yet called Minardi.

Scuderia del Passatore did well in Formula Italia, with Gian Carlo Martini (Pier Luigi's uncle) crowned champion in 1973. Scuderia Everest entered the European Formula Two Championship in 1975 and 1976 with a March BMW.

"It was one of the highlights of my career. I met Enzo Ferrari in 1974. At that time I considered car racing purely a hobby. During the day I tried to sell as many cars I could working for my family's Fiat dealership, and then in the evening, with some of the mechanics, we would manage the Formula Italia and Formula 3 cars, and later, the Formula 2 cars. It was a hobby that suddenly developed into something bigger. Mr de Montezemolo, Ferrari's sporting manager at the time, asked to meet me. He told me "the Commendatore would like to meet you". I answered "whenever you want, I live in Faenza, it's nearby, and in one hour I can be in Maranello". He invited me right away and I spent one full afternoon talking with Enzo Ferrari. I left the smoky meeting with the famous experience of letting young Italian pilots try the 312T model. I brought it to Faenza and that is when my attitude towards car racing changed completely. It started to become a professional interest."

The Scuderia Everest Ferrari hit the track in 1976 and quickly hit problems. Gian Carlo Martini crashed it on the warm-up lap for the Race of Champions at Brands Hatch. You could say they had a mountain to climb.

The F2 outfit later received Dino V6 engines, and in 1979 Minardi became a constructor in his own right, forming the Minardi Team. If you analysed Gian Carlo's blood you'd probably find traces of petrol. The Minardis run the oldest Fiat dealership in Italy and father Giovanni took his young son along to watch him race. Later, Gian Carlo took responsibility for the racing side of the family firm but soon established he wouldn't himself cut it as a driver.

Unsurprisingly, Enzo was Gian Carlo's role model. Yet already the English teams, the teams the Old Man patronised as the 'garagistes' because they didn't build their own engines, were on top in Formula 1. Speaking some English was something Enzo wouldn't contemplate and, frankly, he didn't have to. Gian Carlo now accepts times had changed and, for the good of Minardi, he really should have swallowed his pride and taken some language lessons.

The late 1970s is also when what can only be called a feud began with a young F2 team owner called Ron Dennis. In fact, the mild-mannered Gian Carlo says it is one of his principal regrets in life that in 1978 he didn't punch Ron when he should have.

"I was running Miguel Angel Guerra at Mugello. He ran an extra lap after the chequered flag, although we was shown the sign with an arrow to return to the pit. He made a mistake. When Dennis arrived he offended me, he said 'the same old Italians,' he even added Italian spaghetti. I didn't speak English then and there had been some conflicts between us in the Formula 2 commission meetings. We never really argued. I got really upset under those circumstances, I ran after him with a hammer and they stopped me." Gian Carlo is now laughing hard. [Despite repeated requests, it was not possible to secure an interview with Ron Dennis].

Here's Gian Carlo on Ron's F1 career: "He's had more luck than ability. It's shocking to see what he's been incapable of doing with the budget he's had."[1] That's a little difficult to swallow when one considers McLaren's seven constructor titles under Dennis. Minardi's barb echoes a regular comment made by Ken Tyrrell about Ferrari, so one can see the battle lines.

While Ron got on with Project Four and his takeover of McLaren, young guns like Elio de Angelis and Euro F3 champion Michele Alboreto were driving for Minardi. The 1981 season with Alboreto was its best. Former Maranello engineer Giacomo Caliri became the designer, and he would later pen Minardi's first four cars as an F1 constructor. BMW engines were now prepared by Heini Mader, who would later help Minardi out of a hole in F1. In June '81, 25-year-old Michele took pole on the wonderful French street circuit at Pau, and in July he got on the podium at Enna (alongside Thierry Boutsen and young Dutchman Huub Rothengatter, who would 20 years later manage Minardi driver Jos Verstappen).

Minardi's home race, the Gran Premio dell'Adriatico at Misano on September the 6th 1981, remains the day of days. 25-year-old Michele dominated the field and was nine seconds clear of that season's champion Geoff Lees in his Ralt/Honda.

"The one and only win and the one and only pole position," says Minardi. "We had a series of placements that allowed the team to be in the top three-four in the European championship. Alboreto was a great pilot and a special human being. Besides his racing abilities, he had a unique personality especially regarding human relations; he was always one step ahead. He started professional racing with us. Then almost immediately he ran with Tyrrell. He played a huge role in the history of Italian car racing."

If one needs proof that Gian Carlo was in this for the love of it, consider he was the only F2 team boss to offer a young Ayrton Senna a seat with no financial strings attached. Although he couldn't accept it at the time, it was a kindness Senna would not forget.

Two more Italian hotshots learning their trade at Minardi F2 were Alessandro Nannini and Paolo Barilla, the sons of coffee and pasta dynasties. What could be more Italian? Both would go on to drive for Minardi F1 (as would Alboreto at the end of his career), but in 1982 Misano proved a good F2 track again with Nannini finishing second. He remembers Minardi as the perfect place for his apprenticeship, although feels the BMW engines supplied to Minardi were down on power compared to the March team's.

Michele Alboreto preparing for F2 race. Thruxton, England, 1981.
(Courtesy Sutton Motorsport Images)

1983 confirmed Minardi as 'Misano specialists', with a second on his F2 debut for 22-year-old Pier Luigi Martini. He was also on the verge of being crowned European Formula 3 champion, beating the likes of Gerhard Berger and Emanuele Pirro. There were glimpses of what he could do in F1 when Minardi gave him a good package but it remains a crying shame Martini wasn't able to fulfil his potential.

1984 was the last season for Formula 2. It was to be replaced by the unlamented Formula 3000. But lower formulae tinkering didn't matter; Minardi had already decided to enter the big time.

[1] Interview with Atlas website

1985

I wouldn't start from here ...

The memory of the first Grand Prix is crystal clear; Minardi describes Friday the 5th of April 1985 as "a beautiful day, [that date] means a lot to me. My dad died on the 5th of April and I received the Ferrari engines on the 5th of April 1990."

1985 was slap-bang in the middle of the turbo age; not a great time to try out the normally-aspirated Cosworth. In retrospect, Minardi would have been better off sticking with the venerable DFV but its own turbo was on the way. A team of thirteen, including young driver Pier Luigi Martini, flew to Brazil with the yellow and midnight blue M185. It really was another age. In the 21st century, the big boys take ten times as many staff to races. Gian Carlo Minardi laments that 'progress' as a change for the worse. Martini qualified some 12 seconds off the pole time and retired with electronics problems. The second race in Portugal was much better; Piero qualified within a second of Martin Brundle's Tyrrell, also powered by Cosworth.

It was the arrival of Minardi F1 and Gian Carlo revelled in it and took charge of the front jack: "I think that day [in Brazil] was the best in my motor racing history. Unfortunately, the air you breathe in the garage now is not the one you breathed in those days. The atmosphere is definitely different."[1]

In fact, the omens had been good. Alfa Romeo said it would supply turbo engines, Minardi was a Formula 2 race winner, the Old Man up the road in Maranello was a fan ... come on, let's do it! Then Alfa changed its mind.

"We managed to get [to F1] and it was a beautiful day." The M185 in its first Grand Prix; Rio de Janeiro, 1985. (Courtesy Sutton Motorsport Images)

Several of the original Minardi staff stayed loyal until the very end, including Fagnocchi (2nd from left), Zama (4th), Monti (5th), Manucci (7th), and Sangiorgi (10th) with Minardi on the right. Compare with the 2005 team photo on page 124. (Courtesy Sutton Motorsport Images)

"We asked Mr Massacesi, then president of Alfa Romeo, to provide engines for 1985," recalls Gian Carlo. "We built the first car based on the eight cylinder engine. Then someone waged war against us. Probably we were bothering Euroracing, which was about to disappear. There had been an exchange of letters, an agreement, not a contract. That agreement was already obsolete when we built the car."

Another Italian team, Osella, had put a stop to the V8 deal. It was already the point of no return for Minardi and it re-jigged the chassis to take a Cosworth for the first two races. The only other team doing so was Tyrrell, midway on a long slide from the glory days. In retrospect Minardi thinks he should have stuck with Cosworth, as the cars troubled Tyrrell in those opening races. Two years later the powers-that-be even created the Jim Clark and Colin Chapman trophies for the smaller teams with normally-aspirated Cosworth engines. Jonathan Palmer and Tyrrell won both.

'The Engine Problem' would forever plague Minardi. Rarely was there a big problem with the Faenza cars; indeed, a number of Formula 1 aero and technical revolutions began with Minardi, notably the titanium gearbox and the scooped front-wing. However, the bottom line was always the bottom line with engine deals. The harsh fact is through lack of sponsorship, lack of schmoozing and lack of luck Gian Carlo Minardi failed to get a decent supply.

Pier Luigi Martini. (Courtesy Giorgio Nada Editore)

Ferrari and Alfa engineering legend, Carlo Chiti, formed Motori Moderni. The turbos were not a huge success. (Courtesy Giorgio Nada Editore)

Martini had been drafted by Minardi because Sandro Nannini couldn't get an FISA superlicence. More importantly, admits Sandro, he didn't get the money together. Martini had a superlicence thanks to his outing for Toleman at Monza the previous season, but the call-up to one-car Minardi was a mixed blessing. "It was the only chance I had to drive. No-one else was offering another car in F1."

By Imola, it was time for the turbo, which duly blew up. The engine was a sort of unofficial Alfa as it was designed by ex-Alfa man Carlo Chiti, who formed Motori Moderni along with long-time Minardi associate Piero Mancini. Minardi admits the V6 wasn't up to much, but it was all they had for the next three seasons. "We were a private company who had built a turbo engine pretending to compete with Ferrari, Renault, etc. If someone were to try this today they would be considered crazy."

Martini failed to qualify at Monaco and had an accident in Montreal. This was the pattern until the Nürburgring in August

The new turbo failed after just 14 laps. A sign of things to come. (Courtesy Giorgio Nada Editore)

where the M185 was classified 11th, albeit retired five laps down. The finale in Adelaide was the high point, finishing eighth ... out of eight. Martini was the target of unfair criticism, especially within the team, by people who should have known better. Martini is keen to point out Gian Carlo Minardi was not one of his detractors.

"It was mainly the engine. We couldn't do more than a handful of laps each time and it wasn't letting us develop. Whatever we had – and we didn't have the best – couldn't be developed. I have nearly forgotten 1985 but I know that it was good for me in the sense that I had to understand that one must always fight, without ever losing hope, and without ever stopping that fight. I really try and get positive experience from the past."[2]

Minardi and Martini in the pits at Imola. He qualified 19th out of 26. (Courtesy Giorgio Nada Editore)

Minardi had taken the chequered flag only three times all season, and a shattered Martini took a step down, in terms of series, to F3000. It was a good move, as he finished second to Ivan Capelli in the 1986 championship.

[1] Autosport 31.3.2005
[2] grandprix.com

1986

Nervous breakdown

"I wasn't very glad about Martini getting the drive in 1985," says Alessandro Nannini. "Obviously, I had to wait but they had a lot of problems with the engine. We had the power but it broke almost every time. In '86 I finished just two or three races – usually after ten or fifteen laps it would go." Sandro's memory is being kind. In fact, he had a solitary classified finish; 14th in the penultimate round in Mexico.

Nothing had improved on the technical side. In fact, the mechanics were now worrying about two cars instead of one. Sandro Nannini finally got his F1 break and he was joined by compatriot Andrea de Cesaris. There was no reliability to speak of and neither car qualified at Monaco.

At Spa, de Cesaris ran out of fuel just short of the placings. He had tremendous bad luck but had shaken off his reputation as 'de Crasheris', waiting until Estoril in September for his first accident. 1986 was Minardi's 'annus horribilis' as it had to wait until October for placings. Round fifteen in Mexico was the fifth race for the only M186, and de Cesaris finished eighth, ahead of

Danner, Palmer and Brundle. Nannini came in 14th in the old car. In Adelaide, de Cesaris proved the speed was there by qualifying 11th. Unfortunately, his cockpit fire extinguisher went off halfway through the race and the season was over in a cloud of white dust. Two placings from 29 starts.

Minardi reveals they were running the team on favours, "for turbines, we relied on our friendships, mine with Ferrari and Chiti's with Alfa. Many times they gave us materials that they didn't use which we needed in order to race. It was impossible for us to have access to certain technologies; we didn't have the strength and financial resources."

The positives were behind-the-scenes. Minardi now had use of Ferrari's test track at Fiorano and also Fiat's research facilities. The relationship with Pirelli was good and de Cesaris brought much-needed sponsorship. Minardi's mechanics got a good write-up at Silverstone, too, when they were able to repair Nannini's badly damaged car in time for a re-start.

Quite rightly, much is made of the 'Minardi nursery' for racing drivers, but this tends to overlook the technical side. Engineers and mechanics have gone on to successful careers in many other teams, most notably Gustav Brunner and Aldo Costa. At Faenza, they have worked minor miracles on tiny budgets; for instance, getting the 2005 car ready for Imola. Their pit stop work is exemplary, and Gian Carlo Minardi has admitted thinking about reforming his 'dream team', if only he'd had the money.

Alessandro Nannini in his first F1 race in Rio in March 1986. Technical issues meant he would have to wait until October before his first classified finish. (Courtesy Giorgio Nada Editore)

Andrea de Cesaris was no luckier than his compatriot. At least he came home eighth in Mexico City. (Courtesy Giorgio Nada Editore)

Nannini crashes his M185B at Monza. (Courtesy Giorgio Nada Editore)

1987

Just when you thought ...

"When I signed for Minardi in 1987 he told me they expected to finish on the podium in '89, win races in '90 and fight for the championship in '92," says Adrian Campos. The Spaniard came with high expectations, but, more importantly, sponsorship from clothing giant Lois. "OK, they weren't on the podium in '89 but if you are still the last team in '92 something is very wrong. Then you become the destination for poor drivers and everybody expects Minardi to be last. It was hard for Gian Carlo to get out of this place."

If Minardi thought 1986 was bad, 1987 must have been demoralising. In retrospect, the positive was that it was the last season he was handicapped by a dud turbo. Some mechanics say you could make the Motori Moderni blow up in the garage simply by looking at it. When it worked it was more than 150bhp down on the Honda but, frankly, no-one could keep up so the days of 1000bhp turbos were numbered.

Pirelli withdrew from Grand Prix racing for two years, but Campos says problems with tyres and engines were eclipsed entirely by the gearbox.

"If we went higher than 2.5 bar boost the gears went. The engine easily finished 30% of the races but not the gears – they changed everything every time we went to the track but still it broke. At Hockenheim, I was fourth when the gears went. Johansson got to the end with three tyres [claiming second]. If I'd finished that race I would have been on the podium. It would have changed my life."

Adrian Campos went on to a successful career running his own GP2 team and managing Fernando Alonso. He counts Minardi as one of his closest friends but says his Achilles heel is his lack of English. "I don't speak English like Spanish or Italian but I can speak it with many, many people. For Gian Carlo it is still difficult now. He hardly spoke with Bernie [out of embarrassment]." This is something conceded readily by Minardi and, of course, it meant he had fewer friends and allies in the paddock. "I was pretty much on my own, a mistake on my part, mainly due to language problems. I paid for that mistake."

It's little wonder Nannini signed for Benetton for 1988 as the reliability nightmare continued at Minardi. Before he left, he helped film some wonderful on-board footage at Suzuka for Alain Boisnard's *Lap of the Gods* film, available on DVD. It shows the

Adrian Campos and the M187 debut in Brazil. The only overtaking he did was on the parade lap, shortly before disqualification.
(Courtesy Giorgio Nada Editore)

Campos brought new money to Minardi in 1987 and would bring Alonso in 2001. (Courtesy Giorgio Nada Editore)

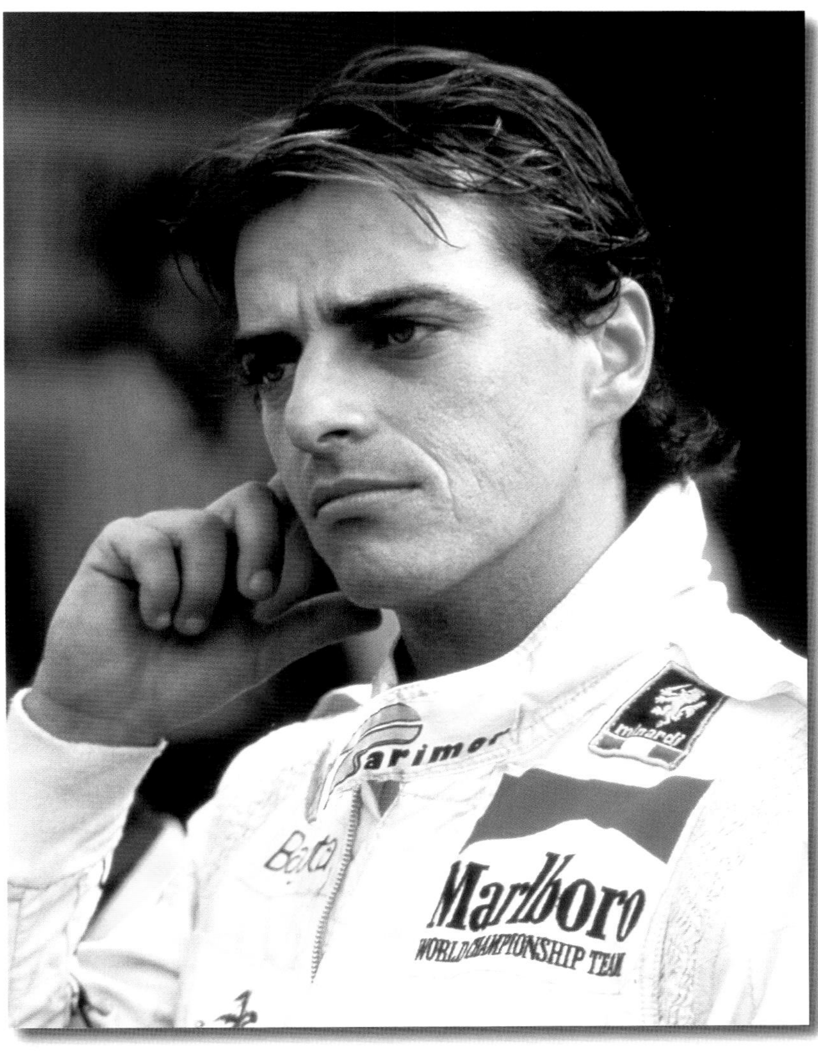

Nannini was again plagued by retirements during his second season with Minardi F1. (Courtesy Giorgio Nada Editore)

Minardi being baulked in practice by Satoru Nakajima on the run up to 130R. Sandro is forced onto the grass but completes the pass shortly before making a cheerful one-fingered wave to the Lotus driver. In the race, Sandro would retire, which can't have been a surprise. Amazingly, just like 1986, he retired from all but one of the races in the '87 season. At the German GP, he was in 7th at halfway when he was forced out.

"It was very, very hard psychologically," he says. "I had to drive as if it was a Le Mans car. Very quiet, very soft, the turbo was very low because of the fuel consumption. I drove like it was Le Mans and then it broke in any case!" Sandro can chuckle now. "When I went to Benetton my head was much better."

He had to wait until round nine at the Hungaroring for his first view of the chequered flag, finishing 11th ahead of Ghinzani and Fabre. At Monza and Estoril the Motori Moderni's thirst was in evidence yet again as he ran dry. At least in terms of official finishes Minardi had doubled its tally to four.

Sponsors were leaving and there was no way Minardi could survive another season like 1987.

The electrics did for Sandro in Monaco ... (Courtesy Giorgio Nada Editore)

... and it was the turbo in Belgium. (Courtesy Giorgio Nada Editore)

1988 Competing

"The new car was completely shit," says Adrian Campos. "I remember the first time testing the M188 at Monza, it was very difficult to keep it in a straight line – the back of the car didn't want to follow the front, it was unbelievable. Sala did 20 laps and said 'I don't want to drive it anymore' and he stopped."

Luis Perez Sala laughs as he confirms the story. "That's true, the car was undriveable and that's why we started to change a lot of things in the team. The new car was worse than the old one. It was very difficult to set up, so inconsistent. Up, down, up, down; not nice to drive." The young Spaniard knew all about good cars and, indeed, Italian teams. He'd been driving for Italian F3 and F3000 outfits for three seasons and was a proven race winner. Luis joining Adrian ensured it was now a case of the Spanish 'in position' at Minardi. Jeans company Lois threw all its eggs in the Minardi basket and one would break before very long.

"The team was not working in the right way," says Luis. "I saw in F3000 with Lola and other teams the level of the organisation you need to fight for wins. Minardi had the talent but not the structure. I was friends with Gian Carlo but I fought a lot with him and the engineers. I said to him during 1988 'you have to change these things or I will leave Formula 1 because I cannot see the light.'"

The person who helped brighten things was new team manager Jaime Manca-Graziadei. "Giacomo Caliri [the designer] was a lovely person but completely out of touch. He didn't have a calculator let alone computers! The car was a shitbox. It was also horrible, all that midnight blue made it look like a hearse."

Manca-Graziadei would more than double a payroll of 34 during his three years at Faenza. He says his main role was to broaden horizons. "I had to get Minardi out of the ghetto. I am British by education so I started talking to all the other teams. I knew Jo Ramirez, Ron Dennis, Ken Tyrrell, Bernie. Before then, Minardi was only talking with Ferrari and the arrogance of those people in Maranello is unforgiveable. Gian Carlo had a special relationship with the Old Man but as soon as Fiat came in it was useless."

"All that midnight blue made it look like a hearse." The M188 at Imola. (Courtesy Giorgio Nada Editore)

Luis Perez Sala impressed immediately. He qualified 15th at Monaco. (Courtesy Giorgio Nada Editore)

start of his team-mate's problems. Campos failed to qualify after crashing with Jonathan Palmer and would also fail to make the cut in Mexico and Canada. The next race was a week later on the streets of Detroit, and Campos was dropped in favour of test driver Pier Luigi ('Piero') Martini. Jaime Manca-Graziadei admits it was an awkward situation as Campos was the 'money man':

"It was pretty difficult to convince him to let go but the guy was not up to Formula 1. The sensation we all had was he was afraid to go fast. He was a gentleman about it, he just let go."

Monaco was the beginning of the end for Adrian Campos. (Courtesy Giorgio Nada Editore)

The design office at Faenza may have been the land that time forgot, but the good news was the Cosworth DFZ prepared by Heini Mader. In 1988, the turbos were regulated and in retreat and almost half the grid was back with Cosworth. Minardi, of course, had been forced to start its debut season with the famous V8, but '88 was a season-long deal and the first of many. It was a good partnership and Cosworth would go on to supply Minardi for all but four of the next 17 seasons.

The drivers' fears were confirmed at Rio when both cars suffered wing failure. At the next race at Imola, Sala finished 11th ahead of, among others, Patrese, Palmer and Gugelmin. The Minardi garage had a star signing too in Ermanno Cuoghi, Niki Lauda's mechanic during his championship years at Ferrari. The third race of the season was Minardi's bogey track, Monaco. Sala qualified 15th out of 26 and this was the

Pier Luigi Martini follows the blue Rial of Andrea de Cesaris on the way to Minardi's first point. Sixth place in the United States Grand Prix, Detroit, 19th June 1988. (Courtesy Sutton Motorsport Images)

Adrian Campos refutes claims he was slow, arguing he matched times with Sandro Nannini in 1987 and outpaced Martini in testing (this is disputed by the Italian). Campos looks back with sadness and some suspicion about the equipment he was given:

"I lost confidence with the team. Someone told me with two Spanish drivers the money from the Italians went and Martini was waiting with some money. In Montreal free practice I was 14th or something like that and for official practice I was 1.5 seconds slower than that time. My question is 'why?' This is not about how fast the driver is, something happened. They wanted the driver to take the decision because they couldn't remove me contractually. When I finished practice I took the steering wheel and gave it to Gian Carlo and said 'drive your car because I don't want to anymore'."

"It wasn't an easy decision to make," admits Minardi. "I made it and I took all responsibility. I spoke with our Spanish sponsor convincing him it was the right course of action. I remember he told me: 'my friend, you must choose'."

Perez Sala backs up his compatriot, to a point: "The team was confused because the car was no good and we didn't have good results. Of course, the drivers are the first people to get blamed. The team was not working in the right direction and it was a pity for Adrian. He had the talent to drive fast ... but he didn't have the professional way to work to be successful in F1, to get people around him."

Pier Luigi Martini did. It can't have hurt that this was the return of the prodigal son, and what a comeback it was on the streets of Detroit, just seven days after the departure of Campos. Martini started 16th and finished 6th, scoring his and the team's first World Championship point. "You can imagine how we touched the sky when we scored our first point," smiles Minardi. Almost as important, Martini was only a lap down on race winner Ayrton Senna. The team had tasted the big time and it was long overdue. Minardi took 52 races to score a point; a record which may never be beaten.

For Martini, it was a case of 'any time, any place, anywhere'. Piero insists he wasn't worried about coming back with Minardi, things had changed, mainly the engine: "After 15 laps I was fifth," laughs Piero. "I remember there were still 45 laps to go until the end. The car was very heavy to drive and I thought 'Oh shit, it's too long!', but there was a big fire inside of me. It was a big result for everybody and it was really the start of my career in Formula 1. I was most worried about the tyres because I didn't change them. I remember the back tyres were completely finished at the

Monza saw another good qualifying effort: Martini was 14th out of 26. (Courtesy Giorgio Nada Editore)

end. Maybe with a pit stop I could have finished fifth. It was a big emotion and for one month every night was a dream."

Jaime Manca-Graziadei: "Piero had a knack of being quick immediately. The problem was he was a little too arrogant but most racing drivers are like that. He was a bit discontinuous during the race. Sala was much more consistent, sometimes he did three or four laps all to the same tenth, but he wasn't as fast as Piero."

Detroit was also a significant track for Cosworth and Minardi old boy Michele Alboreto who had scored the last victory for the famous V8 and Tyrrell five years earlier.

The spirit of renewed optimism at Faenza fostered higher expectations and a much-needed harder edge. Results dipped in the summer and designer Giacomo Caliri was fired in favour of a team of some recently-hired young bucks, led by future technical directors Aldo Costa and Gabriele Tredozi.

Costa would progress to Ferrari in 1995 and help dig Maranello out of a rut, along with Messrs Todt, Brawn, Byrne and Schumacher. He rose to Technical Director at Ferrari and says he owes everything to Gian Carlo Minardi, who displayed great courage hiring a 26-year-old post-graduate mechanical engineer from the University of Bologna. Aldo had cropped up on the radar by collaborating with Ferrari to write an acclaimed thesis on racing suspension but, ironically, there were no openings at Maranello.

"I'd been passionate about Formula 1 since I was 14 but Ferrari was closing its design office [after hiring John Barnard]. There was no possibility here at Maranello so I went into rally cars in Turin with Abarth and the Lancia Delta Integrale. My dream was Formula 1, so as soon as Minardi called me I joined immediately. My dream was to make Minardi a winning team. That's really what I believed. It was very small, I was 33rd on the payroll when I joined!"

Before his rapid promotion to technical director, Aldo Costa focussed on the suspension and Nigel Cowperthwaite of Lotus was drafted in for aerodynamics. "Cowperthwaite designed the only Minardi that ever worked," says Jaime Manca-Graziadei of the following season's far sleeker M189, "it was very simple, pragmatic, typically English. Simple to work on and responsive to changes. The old car you changed everything and it still wouldn't go."

At work, Costa and Cowperthwaite were trying to get the design office out of trouble. It was a far cry from what the young Costa had been learning at Fiat and Ferrari. No proper wind tunnel evaluations, no data acquisition, no consistent methodology. Costa says Minardi was like a 1960s team. "They just hadn't applied modern methodology. I had no problem with Caliri, it was nice to listen to his experience, but Minardi needed to improve his organisation with new fresh people and methodologies."

Sala had a great race at Estoril, finishing eighth, two laps down on winner Alain Prost but ahead of AGS, Ligier, Coloni and, most sweetly, Osella. Adelaide was again kind to Minardi with a seventh for Martini.

But the be all and end all for everyone at Faenza had been achieved on the mean streets of Detroit with little Piero. Yes, a World Championship point meant more money, the FOCA travel benefits of free long-haul freight and exemption from the dreaded pre-qualifying, but more than all of that, Minardi was now competing in Formula 1, not simply existing.

1989

Leading

Almost by definition, people very rarely appreciate 'the golden years' at the time. They're too busy enjoying the present, and anyway, the future might be even better. Hindsight tells us these are Minardi's golden years.

1989 would be full of worry about being relegated to the ranks of pre-qualifying; literally a twilight world where the likes of Onyx, EuroBrun and Zakspeed fought for the right to take part in the main qualifying session. 1989 would also see a double points finish, a Minardi actually leading a lap of a race and the team's best chance of a win dashed by a downpour Down Under.

Spanish sponsor Lois kept the faith, so Minardi had stability in the driver line-up. The sleek M189 was Aldo Costa's first of seven at Faenza and Pirelli returned to Formula 1 with Minardi its top team. The tyres could be fantastic and helped Martini qualify an excellent 11th at Imola and Monaco. Later in the season he even got onto the second row at Jerez and Adelaide.

Perez Sala confirms the new car was a massive improvement, but the inconsistency of the tyres proved a major handicap. "It was a disaster. [There were severely limited supplies] and we didn't even know what tyres we were getting so setup was impossible. Each time they changed the tyres, they didn't say what it was. To run like that during a weekend was very difficult to understand. Pirelli tried to invest a lot of money making different compounds and many didn't work, but we still had to use them! The Pirellis worked quite well at Silverstone and I had a good choice because after warm-up the Pirelli people said 'look, we have Piero test a good set in warm-up, this is the one you should use but we only have three sets.' The first time they said something to me about that – it was the eighth race of the season and only now was I understanding the problem! They said we can give one set to Pier Luigi, one to

Luis Perez Sala. (Courtesy Giorgio Nada Editore)

you Luis and the other one to Stefano Modena or another guy. I was thinking 'why, why, why do they have only three sets?' For the race, I just preferred to use Pier Luigi's set from warm-up ... and they say OK!" Luis laughs a rueful laugh now; how farcical to send someone out like that but, as he says, Pirelli was tackling the might of Goodyear and trying to cover all bases.

Silverstone proved to be the high water mark with a double points finish; fifth for Martini and sixth for Perez Sala. Six cars took the chequered flag after the Minardis, including the Williams of Thierry Boutsen and the Arrows of Derek Warwick. Piero will never forget it, saying it was like going from 'the stables to the stars' ('dalle stalle alle stelle').

"The original Italian saying is 'dalle stelle alle stalle', which people say when everything has gone wrong; from the stars to the stables. But at Silverstone the exact opposite occurred."

His recollection of the race is enthusiastic: "I had to stop for overheating problems, but then I did well by recovering to fifth place, also dragging Sala to sixth behind me ... I passed Sala and with my hand I was saying 'come on, come on, follow me!' It was a strange race for everybody. It was a big success because it was our last chance to avoid pre-qualifying. I made 16 points with Minardi and every point for me has been a victory."

Sala: "Pier Luigi had problems and then he overtook me for fifth and I say 'fantastic, he's fifth, I'm sixth, unbelievable' and I had

Arms folded, Gian Carlo Minardi watches Martini prepare to leave the garage. (Courtesy Giorgio Nada Editore)

Opposite: Pier Luigi Martini in 1989. (Courtesy Giorgio Nada Editore)

Sala racing to sixth at Silverstone during Minardi's day of days. (Courtesy Giorgio Nada Editore)

Olivier Grouillard behind me fighting for sixth place and I couldn't see him properly because of my dirty mirrors! I didn't know where he was quicker than me but it was a very nice race and when I saw the flag it was a fantastic feeling. The most beautiful thing was it was a party for the whole team, both sides of the garage." Sala laughs about avoiding pre-qualifying "it was like a miracle for the team ... and for a Spanish driver to get a point [back then] was like the world title."

Jaime Manca-Graziadei recalls the tension: "I remember the evening before we were having dinner at the hotel and Mike Earle of Onyx was at the next table celebrating with champagne because they were going to take our spot and I thought 'I wouldn't drink that champagne quite yet.' The next day we fucked them up but he was the first one to congratulate us. It was a lucky escape at the last minute."

To the amazement of the Ferrari contingent, a welcoming party awaited the Minardi team at Bologna airport. Nigel Mansell may have finished second for Ferrari but that's first of the losers as far as the Tifosi is concerned.

Aldo Costa, later one of the top men at Maranello, chuckles at the memory of passing through the airport, "The Ferrari guys didn't understand too much what was going on, it was a great day ... for us it was really a victory." If one omits the 'race' at Indianapolis 2005, it was to be the only time in Minardi's history both cars got into the points at a Grand Prix.

Minardi's tremendous formation finish at Silverstone was

"Dalle stalle alle stelle." Forza Minardi!
(Courtesy Giorgio Nada Editore)

A lap at the front for the M189. Minardi leads the Portuguese Grand Prix.
(Courtesy Sutton Motorsport Images)

repeated at Monza, just outside the points. At the next race, Pier Luigi Martini actually led a lap of the Portuguese Grand Prix. OK, others were pitting but the record book doesn't lie. For 2.7 miles, Minardi was P1. Martini had qualified fifth and that's how he finished, ahead of his team-mate and eight others.

Seasoned F1 writer Joe Saward reported at the time "There is a massive closet Minardi fan club in the paddock. Everyone loves the underdog; to see the little guys sticking two fingers up to the big guys and making them squirm."[1]

Actually, even the 'big guys' were fans. "I remember Saturday night at Jerez," says Manca-Graziadei. "We had fourth on the grid for the next day; I was wandering around in the paddock and out of the dark Ron Dennis jumps at me, with his usual hard attitude telling me that we were causing him problems. I was taken aback as I did not really know what we'd done wrong, so he tells me that he was negotiating with Honda the following year's contract and that they were adamant at not giving him the money he wished because 'all that money for just being half a second in front of Minardi, with their little budget, was unjustified'. He then looked at me and smiled and patted me on the shoulder and said: 'I know Gian Carlo does not like me but you chaps are doing a terrific job, well done.'"

Aldo Costa recalls the season with affection, astonishment and a chuckle:

"We were very, very young.

Unbelievably young! I was 27-28 and probably one of the oldest engineers. OK, there was Tomasso Carletti as well, let's say our 'big father' but the team was very, very young and very motivated. A lot of people coming from outside Faenza and I remember a very nice environment. We used to go out each night, eating together. It was a really nice, dynamic team. I have to say that Gian Carlo was very brave to give to me first the responsibility to design the car and then to become technical director with so very little experience.

"My opinion of Pier Luigi was very, very positive, of course. He was very fast for the qualifying lap, he was a really fast driver and what we enjoyed was, even in the free practice he was slightly slower sometimes, we knew that he had in his pocket his final lap and when the time was right he came out with his final lap. Very, very quick. And I had a very good technical relationship with Martini because he was able to transfer to me the car feeling and the car behaviour so we did a very good job together. For me, his presence in the team was very important."

Piero suffered a broken rib at Jerez; not on the track, but in the paddock. He fell down the steps of the team truck. Ex-Minardi F2 driver Paolo Barilla subbed at Suzuka (a race rather more famous for an all-McLaren tangle).

Martini was back with a bang for Adelaide's controversial 'monsoon' Grand Prix. In dry qualifying he secured a fabulous third on the grid, but sadly the Pirellis were nowhere near as good in the wet. Standing water led to new champion Alain Prost trying in vain to get the start delayed. After a tentative getaway for all, Martini had a hairy moment, but he kept it on the road behind the McLaren duo. Prost, of course, famously retired at the end of the first lap and the inevitable red flags came out after a crash.

Piero had a very good second start yet the Pirelli wets were no use at all, and Senna soon pulled away. The Williams cars got by and Thierry Boutsen would eventually win the two hour 'race'. The non-existent visibility caused many spins and some horrible crashes; Piero was a fortunate bystander to the Piquet/Ghinzani accident and eventually finished sixth, albeit three laps down.

"I was first in the warm-up, maybe without rain it could have been our best opportunity to win the race. Our tyres were not good enough in the wet – at the end of the race they still looked brand new! The other Pirelli cars were impossible to drive. Just going in a straight line was difficult. Stefano Modena had the same tyres on his Brabham and I lapped him three times. Qualifying in the dry had been perfect, every corner was on the limit, it was a fantastic lap."

Minardi rues the deluge. "It was our most important opportunity and we blew it but it wasn't our fault. I stopped Piero in the warm-up as he had the best time after 16 minutes. Maybe that day we could have achieved the best ever result. A sunny morning which turned into a flooded afternoon, maybe it was just bad luck. Probably achieving a better result during that race, considering certain advertising investments and main team decisions Pirelli was about to make, would have changed our history."

Minardi's partnership with Pirelli had been very productive and Martini says it was crucial to their great season. The driver was certainly getting noticed by other teams but he decided to stay with Minardi and build on the momentum. What he didn't realise was that the tyre company had decided to focus its efforts on Tyrrell.

The M189 was far more competitive than its successor in 1999, but things tend to even themselves out. A decade after the near miss at Adelaide, Minardi adapted well to changeable conditions at the Nürburgring as others fell by the wayside. Johnny Herbert won that race for Stewart; back in 1989 he finished joint 14th in the championship, alongside a certain Pier Luigi Martini.

For the constructors, Minardi finished with six points yet remained tenth in the table. Sala left Formula 1 after just two seasons and that solitary point at Silverstone. "Look, at the end I wanted to be in F1 to fight for victory, not to just stay there. After two years showing my speed, my talent, what I showed to the team managers was not enough to improve my position. The only opportunities I had were in the same sort of car or even worse and that didn't make sense." He didn't have a big sponsor, and of those pre-Alonso years says "for a Spanish driver to get into Formula 3 was successful," let alone Formula 1. His compatriots were, back then, far more interested in motorbikes and rally cars. "I could not stay with Minardi but it was very nice, I was living there for two years, training with Pier Luigi, they were like my second family. Despite the bad times, I have very nice memories." The ever-philosophical Luis pursued a career in touring cars.

[1] grandprix.com

1990

Phoenix nights

It may seem ridiculous now, but Ayrton Senna was toying with the idea of joining Minardi. One well-placed source reveals Ayrton went as far as saying “I want to prove to everyone how good I am” when his time was up at McLaren. He was fed-up with the politics and made many late night phone calls to Gian Carlo Minardi. Senna enjoyed his furtive visits to the Minardi canteen (Ron didn’t approve – he and Gian Carlo still nursing grudges from ‘hammer time’ at Mugello in 1978) and even had plates of pasta sent up to him at McLaren. But could he have really signed with Minardi? “Senna used to say this and also his dad repeated it quite often,” smiles Gian Carlo. “We had a great friendship. He often secretly came to visit us to eat spaghetti; his dad was always in our motor home. He used to say on several occasions, jokingly I believe, that he wanted to win the famous five world titles or more to equal and beat Fangio and then he would race his last year with us to end his career. In 1982, I offered him to race in F2 and I was the only one, he said, that didn’t ask him for money, but actually was willing to pay him.”

Martini follows Berger on the parade lap at Phoenix. Sixteen years later Gerhard would become co-owner of the Faenza team. (Courtesy Sutton Motorsport Images)

Three World Championships at McLaren were followed by a switch to Williams. Ayrton Senna had to wait, though, while Alain Prost secured his fourth and final title in 1993. We will never know if Senna would really have driven for Minardi. It certainly appealed to a mischievous nature. More seriously, it would have showcased his talent and, as Gian Carlo Minardi admits, 'it's a nice dream'.

The new decade started well but, in reality, 1990 saw Minardi take a step back to the bad old days. Come the end of the season there were no points on the board.

Round one in Phoenix promised much. Faster than Senna and Prost, the sticky Pirellis helped Martini qualify second alongside the McLaren of pole-sitter Gerhard Berger, the man he had beaten to the Euro F3 title. Piero said at the time how satisfying it was to show what he could do and the press room rocked with cheers.

"At that time a small team with a good car, a good engine and competitive tyres could achieve those results. That success is not repeatable in today's F1. That's why I feel a bit gloomy comparing those days to the present."[1]

It would be Minardi's only front row and a distant memory during the final years of toil. Martini finished just outside the points in a race remembered for Alesi's epic battle with Senna. From then on, Pirelli certainly switched its focus to Tyrrell.

Cramp forced the retirement of the other Minardi driver less than 20 laps from the end. Pasta-heir Paolo Barilla had brought sorely-needed sponsorship from the family firm and had driven for Minardi in F2, where he was rather over-shadowed by Alessandro Nannini. In Minardi F1 he was eclipsed by Martini and failed to qualify at six tracks, leading many observers to assume he was out of his depth. However, Paolo couldn't have been a dud – he'd won Le Mans in 1985 in a Joest Porsche. Minardi tech boss Aldo Costa reveals the pain behind the lack of performance and that cramp at Phoenix. "I am still a bit sorry

Paolo Barilla and Gian Carlo Minardi. Poor Paolo was cramped inside the M190. (Courtesy Giorgio Nada Editore)

about Paolo. At that time, the cars were very narrow, there were no minimal dimensions for the cockpit so we were all doing them smaller and smaller and we ended up with a cockpit that was too small for him. I remember him suffering and, retrospectively, it was a shame. He's a tall guy with big shoulders and it was very difficult to race."

Ferrari tester Gianni Morbidelli replaced Barilla for the final two GPs and, despite qualifying, retired from both. He'd done enough to stay on with Martini for the next season. Ace designer Nigel Cowperthwaite was off, though, to Scuderia Italia.

What was the difference with 1989? Costa says the development budget was never stable; he simply didn't know how much money he had to play with: "For a few years we were fluctuating, oscillating from having good money and having no money, so the programmes suffered. We couldn't

Pier Luigi bent his M190 at Imola. (Courtesy Giorgio Nada Editore)

The M190 at Monza. "We couldn't have a consistent, continuous pushing programme." Aldo Costa. (Courtesy Giorgio Nada Editore)

have a consistent, continuous pushing programme. So there was a good push for '89 but then we had a problem and had to reduce the money. Then a good push for '91 but then in the middle of the season we had to come back. It was going a bit too much up and down."

Minardi's own analysis includes a fair dollop of bad luck. "It was a sequence of events. We took the risk of building a new car. As a small team it wasn't easy. We started with the 1989 car [M189] and we reached the pole position in Phoenix. Then we tried the new car [M190 at the home race Imola], maybe paying the price for different choices made by our tyre supplier. In 1990, a major team partnered with Pirelli. There were several events that didn't help the team. We were already focussed on the Ferrari engines which were supposed to become our next significant improvement."

Team manager Jaime Manca-Graziadei sees it differently. Even though Enzo Ferrari was long gone, he argues Gian Carlo was sentimental about links with Maranello. "It was a big mistake; he should have gone with the Britishers. I had been working all of 1989 to get the Ford factory deal and we had a great contract in our hands. It was the engine which eventually went to Jordan and look at what they did in '91. I discovered Gian Carlo was going to Maranello too often and when I confronted him in February '90 he confessed he was working on an engine deal with Cesare Fiorio. He was doing it all on his own very secretively. I told him I was out if he signed but he went ahead. [I was proven right] because they gave him a three year old engine, charged twice as much as Ford would have for a factory deal and even took our Pioneer sponsorship."

From the outside, one would have expected 1991 to be the breakthrough.

[1] Interview with Minardi Club San Francisco (minardiusa.com)

1991

Seventh heaven

Echoing Enzo in the 1970s, Ferrari technical director Cesare Fiorio firmly believed Minardi should act as Maranello's nursery. Fiorio would later join Minardi but in 1991 he ensured a supply of Ferrari V12s for the M191.

The downside of being a junior team is that big brother can do what he wants. Pioneer sponsorship was small fry for Ferrari but they took it anyway. They also reclaimed Morbidelli who, when he finished races for Minardi, finished well. He was promoted to race for Ferrari in the final round after the sacking of Alain Prost. Brazilian 'super sub' Roberto Moreno deputised at Minardi following his shafting at Benetton (one M Schumacher had been brought into the fold).

The star for Minardi, once more, was Pier Luigi Martini. Two fourth places at Imola and Estoril cemented his and Minardi's best season. Eleventh in the drivers' championship and seventh in the constructors'. Piero rates it as his best season in F1 but something funny was going on with the Ferrari engine.

"I finished behind Patrese, Senna and Alesi at Estoril. Schumacher and Piquet were behind me. The race after in Barcelona the engine was so slow, I don't know why but the biggest problem we had with those engines was the gearbox and the clutch. It was only supposed to have an automatic box and we didn't have that at Minardi."

No matter, Martini's big break had come. He signed for a Ferrari drive in 1992 and all was going well until Piero Ferrari lost control of the family firm. "When you are Italian you believe in Ferrari," says Martini. "I believed too much. That was my big mistake." Ferrari switched him with Ivan Capelli, who had been due to drive for Scuderia Italia.

For Minardi too, this is the turning point. This is when Gian Carlo Minardi should have capitalised with bigger sponsorship. He admits he failed but denies Manca-Graziadei's claim that the Ferrari motor was three years old.

"No, I don't think so; they were just one step behind theirs. It was a simple problem. It was an error of judgment on my side. In 1990, I paid 1.5 billion lira for the Mader/Cosworth engines and then I paid 11 billion for the Ferrari engine. The other mistake I made was to enter into several contracts in order to get this engine, which ultimately prevented me from signing other sponsors. I will give you an example: my team wasn't allowed to compete with Marlboro.

Ferrari power for the M191. (Courtesy Giorgio Nada Editore)

Martini, Minardi and Morbidelli launch the M191. Aldo Costa in on the far left. (Courtesy Giorgio Nada Editore)

I can't say how much but what they paid us was ridiculous. Benson & Hedges was willing to pay a lot of money. Another extremely damaging contract stated we couldn't use gasoline other than the brand used by Ferrari which was Agip. I believe they paid us 250 million lira plus free gasoline and consider that in 1993 I signed a contract with Agip which paid me 2.5 billion. When I signed the contract I had put in place a series of deals that vanished later. I had an agreement with Pioneer for a three year sponsorship and instead Pioneer chose Ferrari."

It would be very easy to be judgmental here, yet he is a man trying to do the best for his team, in the considerable shadow of Maranello. The Minardi boy who went on to become Ferrari's Technical Director, Aldo Costa, says the red team has changed. "In my opinion it was silly. Ferrari at that time was unable to get results. They were scared of their own shadow. It was really important for them that Minardi was not a competitor, for sure. None of us realised until it was too late. Unfortunately, in those days Maranello was very, very different from now. Now, between our engine and the customer engine the specification is the same, the difference probably oscillates three horsepower, something like that, because we have to supply good engines to the customer. We want him to make as many points as he can. We want the customer to be satisfied. Back then, it was completely different. They supplied us the Nigel Mansell engine type at the first race, so it was probably two years old." Costa confirms Martini's fears about the engine post-Estoril: "During the season they gave us a step of development in the engine and in the fuel to keep us a very far distance from them. I remember all of a sudden the fuel as we were in Estoril very, very close to them, the fuel became just a standard fuel, instead of being a special fuel which everybody was using at the time, so we lost a lot of horsepower. It was a very bad supply."

It's interesting to note that after its debut season in F1, Jordan managed to attract title sponsorship from SASOL. Gian Carlo Minardi blames himself and his lack of English for the dearth of sponsors. He also blames Italian companies for failing to look beyond the scarlet of Maranello.

Having bled Faenza dry, the money wasn't there for another year of Ferrari. A disillusioned Martini had been shunted to rivals Scuderia Italia Dallara, a path already trodden by aerodynamicist Nigel Cowperthwaite. Dallara had finished behind Minardi in the '91 championship but it had a 'new' engine for '92. A Ferrari. Gian Carlo's been roughed-up a few times in business and he's got the bruises to prove it. "I want to note Minardi had six points and was the top team with Ferrari engines. Scuderia Italia behind us had only two points and Sauber spent four years before it scored more than seven points."

Minardi says with the Ferrari engine deal he thought he'd turned the world around but, in fact, "the world had turned around on me".

Minardi survived in Formula 1 for 21 years. The best was 1991, year seven. It's fair to say the teenage years were 'difficult'.

1992

Power slide

“The sound of the Lamborghini engine was beautiful; it was God’s greatest gift to motor racing in my opinion. It was also big, heavy, made the car use a lot of tyres and it wasn’t even very reliable.”

Christian Fittipaldi, the young Brazilian with the Italian name and the world champion pedigree, joined Minardi for 1992. He was reigning F3000 champion and brought a budget of almost $1.5m.

“Gian Carlo was passionate – I can see it in my Dad (Wilson) and my Uncle (Emerson); those guys are passionate because they come from a different type of racing where the commercial side wasn’t as big as nowadays and they just love racing. I put Gian Carlo, for sure, in the same category. You could see like, shit, how excited he got when you have a good result and even if it wasn’t a points-paying position, like P7, P8, P9, whatever, but he saw you were really trying your very best and the car was maxed out, nothing more could be done that weekend, he was happy.

“There are years in Formula 1 when you get more openings, [but] my year there were virtually no openings at all. There were 34 F1 cars because of pre-qualifying. Minardi had a pretty solid campaign in ’91 and I thought they would have progressed and we started talking and I thought it was a good midfield team to start in Formula 1.”

Fittipaldi didn’t have much luck with the M191B in his first few races but his team-mate, Morbidelli, was just outside the points at Interlagos. Ferrari’s test driver came seventh in the third race of the season.

The M192 debuted at Minardi’s home race, Imola, then Christian showed what he was made of during the ultimate test, the

The M192 debuts at Imola. (Courtesy Giorgio Nada Editore)

Christian Fittipaldi with his uncle Emerson. (Courtesy Giorgio Nada Editore)

Fittipaldi's first season was beset by problems; he retired here at Imola. (Courtesy Giorgio Nada Editore)

Monaco Grand Prix weekend. He got an eighth before a big shunt at Magny-Cours in July. "I had never seen Monaco, unlike other drivers who'd done F3 there. On Thursday morning I had a pretty big accident at the swimming pool. I qualified pretty much at the back. At Magny-Cours, it was starting to drizzle, I don't know if it was that or I just lost it but I went into the wall backwards and I broke my C5 vertebra and cracked my C4. I pretty much saw stars and that was it, I was out of action in a neck brace for two months." Alessandro Zanardi deputised for Christian, who admits he returned too soon, "When I started driving again I was really weak. To be honest, those next two races (Spa and Monza) I didn't qualify and it wasn't a problem with the car, I knew it was a problem with me. I wasn't ready for it, I came back too early."

Fittipaldi out-qualified his more experienced team-mate three times in the opening four races, and he says Morbidelli was his stiffest competition during his time in Formula 1, "when everything was perfect for him and his driving style he was very competitive." They would later team up at Footwork-Arrows in 1994. Morbidelli qualified very well in Monaco and Canada – 12th and 13th compared to Fittipaldi's 17th and 25th. But it was Christian who scored Minardi's only point of 1992.

"At Estoril, something clicked and we were very competitive. At Suzuka, I qualified 12th and was sixth in the race with a Ferrari behind the whole time. It just started rolling again, back to the normal Christian again!

It was good, especially after everything I'd been through that year with the neck injury."

Nicola Larini's Ferrari along with the other Minardi, both Footworks and both Dallaras were among those behind Fittipaldi. But it was Scuderia Italia Dallara that crucially took tenth in the constructors' championship. It had achieved two sixth places early in the season with its Ferrari engine. The driver in the points on both occasions was one Pier Luigi Martini who, it turned out, was on another sabbatical from Minardi. Bernie Ecclestone wouldn't be writing any cheques for Minardi, which was joint eleventh with Jordan and Larrousse.

"I met all my obligations," says Gian Carlo Minardi. "We reduced the engine supply; the 11 billion lira to Ferrari went down to only nine for Lamborghini. But that decision heavily affected us during the following years. In 1993, I had to start selling. We started to face big problems and I signed an agreement with Scuderia Italia."

Most people close to Gian Carlo Minardi believe his lack of English was a handicap in terms of wheeler-dealing and building alliances in the paddock. Indeed, Minardi himself agrees. Interestingly, the boss of bosses, Ecclestone, goes against the grain on this one.

Good-looking swine! Fittipaldi and Nannini have both featured in surveys on F1 pin-ups. (Courtesy Giorgio Nada Editore)

Christian retired with an oil fire in Canada. The next race would see him badly hurt. (Courtesy Giorgio Nada Editore)

Christian's comeback from injury at Spa was too soon. He didn't qualify. (Courtesy Giorgio Nada Editore)

"I don't think his lack of English was critical. English is an nternational language, isn't it, but I don't think that held him back with anything."

Interesting because Ecclestone is the man who anglicised he atmosphere of Grand Prix racing, with a little help from Colin Chapman, Ken Tyrrell, Frank Williams and Ron Dennis. The European Old Guard, the French and the Italians, looked on with FISA-FOCA battle of the early eighties was decided as soon as Bernie was allowed to go off and sort out the commercial deals on behalf of the constructors. So, by the time Gian Carlo Minardi arrived on the scene, English was, if you'll excuse the pun, the lingua franca of F1. Yet Ecclestone believes the Achilles heel was Italian sponsorship. There is only room for one team in Italy, and a lack of home support certainly held back Minardi.

The M192 at Spa. (Courtesy Giorgio Nada Editore)

1993

Monza flip

"It would have been a beautiful podium [to climb] because Prost won, Senna finished second, I would have finished third. What an honour to be together with those two guys on the podium." Close but no champagne for the first race of the season at Kyalami. Christian Fittpaldi finished fourth, the last time a Minardi driver would get that close to a podium. "I didn't know that but I think I'm the driver who scored the most points per starts for Minardi." He's right. Six points in 24 starts for Minardi meant he scored an average of every four races, compared to an average of every six races for Martini (16 points from 102 starts). Fabrizio Barbazza had a similar strike rate to Fittipaldi, scoring two points in just eight starts. Christian doesn't make a big deal out of it as, of course, it's a rather facile comparison, a sidenote. His two seasons with Minardi came at the end of the team's purple patch whereas Piero's long Minardi career spanned all sorts of cars and all sorts of luck.

"'93 was actually pretty good," says Christian. "We had very little money, believe it or not we had less money than in '92. Gustav [Brunner] came on board and between Gustav and Aldo they came up with a pretty decent little car out there on the track."

It was also painted white and many Minardi fans blanched. For them, Minardis should be yellow and midnight blue, or 'blu notte'. Larrousse had sole use of the Lamborghinis so, courtesy of the Briatore/Walkinshaw axis, Minardi was supplied with some Cosworths from the Jaguar sports car campaign.

Kyalami, admittedly, was a race with a mere five finishers but Fittipaldi and his Minardi-Cosworth M193 kept plugging away from 13th on the grid while others crashed or broke down. Team-mate Fabrizio Barbazza scored consecutive sixth place finishes at Donington Park and Imola – the former GP remembered for

Was the M193 the best Minardi? Gian Carlo believes so, Aldo Costa sort of agrees. Fittipaldi almost made the podium in its first race. (Courtesy Giorgio Nada Editore)

Senna's greatest drive. "Barbazza didn't stop as much as me. Five or six stops didn't turn out the right option for me. He did a very good job, he was solid, consistent, I was happy for the team but still I finished 7th ... I even spun once or twice! We were strong all weekend. I qualified 16th, I remember Derek Warwick was ahead of me. You have to remember there were 25 cars in those days."

Christian remembers Senna lapping him at Donington but does he remember the older Brazilian helping him in the paddock? "Yeah,

Fabrizio Barbazza. Crazy name, crazy hair, crazy guy. (Courtesy Giorgio Nada Editore)

he offered advice but we were never really that close. There's no doubt that I listened to everything he said, especially coming from him and having the experience he had ... in a way, we were two worlds apart."

Ayrton would win at Monaco in 1993 with Christian finishing fifth; another great result after qualifying 17th.

"I don't know why but I've always loved Monaco, I've always lapped very well there. 8th, then 5th and in 1994 with Footwork I was running second or third when we had a gearbox problem. In '93, I actually passed three cars; Herbert, Rubens and Alliot on the first or second lap of the race, passed them on the track which I thought was pretty like 'wow!', passing there is very hard. I passed all of them going into the Loews hairpin. I didn't have to stop for tyres, I just kept on going. I remember Brundle stopped for tyres and then at the end of the race my tyres were completely knackered and his Ligier was lapping like two seconds a lap quicker than I was. He was just gaining on me, gaining on me big time, and then the last two laps, it was hell, I really had to make my car very, very wide and he didn't manage to get by," laughs Christian.

If there were points for ingenious crashes, Pier Luigi Martini and Christian would surely have banked ten at Monza. Martini had made another comeback to replace Barbazza and at the end of the Italian Grand Prix was assaulted on the line by Fittipaldi, or is there more to it than that? Martini was in seventh place so the fight for position was literally pointless. Maybe it was down to pride as Fittipaldi launched over the back of Martini's car, did a full flip and

"The points were earned on the tracks and there were no gifts." Gian Carlo Minardi on 1993. (Courtesy Giorgio Nada Editore)

The Minardis come together at Monza in one of F1's weirdest finishes. (Courtesy Sutton Motorsport Images)

as soon as I come out of his slipstream you can see his car move to the same side I was going. I really didn't expect him to move the car, especially after I committed myself out of his draft but that's the way it went. I agree with him, it's a miracle and I'm happy to be here talking to you."

It's clear from what you're saying that you think he backed off ...

"Well, I dunno. I was so happy that I was alive that even if he backed off, I don't give a shit. It's a unique crash because I finished the race. I had no problem with Martini; he obviously knew everybody at

Fittipaldi somehow crosses the line the right way up and in eighth place. (Courtesy Giorgio Nada Editore)

somehow landed on his remaining three wheels. Both reached the flag but Piero reached it first.

"I was very quick and fifth at one point but I lost fifth gear. Christian tried to pass me on the last lap but I didn't let him. I know Monza very well and in the last 200 metres we had a little touch and he flew! He was very lucky, it was a miracle." Note the "I didn't let him."

Christian says the crash was weird: "The only thing that I found really strange was the differential in speed when we had the contact was pretty big and I know it's on the telemetry ... this never became official but the differential in speed was 20km/h and I wasn't going 20km/h quicker than him ..."

So he backed off?

"Well, I don't know. Inside my heart I definitely don't want to think that he did. The other thing is if you look at the TV footage,

Minardi because he had driven there so many years so he had his little crowd but I didn't have any problems with him. I don't have nothing against the guy. Would I go out for a meal with him? No, I wouldn't. I don't hate him but I don't like him."

Apart from the aberration of Indianapolis 2005, 1993 was Minardi's best season for points and Gian Carlo believes the M193 was the best car to bear his name, "It was the first phase with Gustav Brunner, I had an extraordinary staff. Brunner, Aldo Costa, Gabriele Tredozi. A great working team. We had a nice car, we scored seven points, we competed on equal terms with other teams, the points were earned on the tracks and there were no gifts. One of my regrets, besides not speaking English, is that if I had managed to sign up a few more sponsors, maybe, considering the great people we have given away to other teams, we could have created a really strong team."

Technical director in 1993, Aldo Costa, says it may have been weak on budget but it was strong on methodology and that meant strong reliability, as demonstrated in the early races. "I think the '89 car was probably the fastest Minardi because it was combined with the developments from Pirelli; '93 was probably the more consistent car even if it was not the fastest, in my opinion, compared to the competitors, of course."

Seven points only secured eighth place in the final constructor standings, partly explaining why 1991 is regarded as the better year. Another reason is that 1993 saw Gian Carlo Minardi lose control of his team. Seriously strapped for cash, he sold two thirds of the equity to Italian steel tycoon Beppe Lucchini, who was running down his unsuccessful Scuderia Italia project. It was a sort of merger which sort of worked. The team would be entered as Minardi-Scuderia Italia; it remained essentially Minardi but with new money. Gian Carlo was general director and Faenza remained the base.

In fact, money was so tight in the wake of the Ferrari engine deal that Fittipaldi lost his seat for the final races in Japan and Australia. He says Jean-Marc Gounon paid $500,000 for the privilege. It was a frustrating end to Christian's two years at Minardi. Everyone thought the team was going to make the great leap forward in 1993. "I'm not upset but I was obviously expecting a little bit more from the second year. I'm not pointing fingers at anyone, it just went how it went but I really thought the car we had

and with a strong start to the season ... I really thought we would have had a pretty strong season and scored between 10 and 15 points. Unfortunately, it didn't happen that way. I really wanted that to happen for myself and for Minardi but it didn't happen. From the middle of the year onwards things started getting a little bit more hectic, it wasn't flowing and Gian Carlo started having big money problems to the point that they got me out of the car. I really didn't want it to end that way."

Christian turned down a test drive at McLaren before a final year in Formula 1 with Footwork-Arrows. He denies he's envious of the Minardi drivers who made it into bigger teams. "I think, in a way, I made Minardi work for me … I learned a lot with it, I had some good strong runs to the point that in August 1994 I was sitting with Carl Haas at his house on the Tuesday before the Hungarian Grand Prix and I almost struck a deal with them to drive the car for '95. He saw what I'd done and that's why he called me. I almost started racing in America with Newman-Haas but then there were a lot of sponsor conflicts ... but it worked out for '96. I don't look back. I can look at Alonso and Webber and Fisichella, yeah, you can look at it that way, there's no doubt in my mind that Formula 1 is the pinnacle of motor racing. It went the way it went. Sometimes I don't have a lot of patience and I wasn't willing to keep listening to the people talking to me. A lot of people are just big BS-ers [bullshitters], 'we're going to do that, we're going to do this'. Lots of promises that don't go anywhere. When I came over to Champ Car you could realistically qualify P20, P22 and win the race because you were quickest. This fascinated me, this was true racing although, technically speaking, the cars are less advanced than Formula 1. My idea was only to stay here for one or two years and then go back to Formula 1 ... then I signed again with Carl and when I looked back like, shit, seven years had gone by!"

Autocourse included Christian and the M193 in its top ten of driver/car combinations for 1993, and he stayed in touch with Faenza. Like all Minardi boys, he has great affection for Gian Carlo and the staff.

"We met up at Interlagos in 2005 and spent like an hour and a half talking, I saw the bunch of guys still working from when I was there. Honestly, I have good memories, no major regrets, it just went the way it went and I was happy I was part of the family there. By the way, of all the teams I raced with, Minardi is for sure the one that did the best food!"

Christian is not the only F3000 champion to have driven in F1 with Minardi. There's also Luca Badoer, Roberto Moreno and Justin Wilson. Much derided now, there's no doubt the F3000 championship was a tough contest although it's an anomaly that no F3000 champion has ever gone on to lift the big prize in Formula 1 (to the Minardi drivers you can add Montoya, Alesi and Panis).

Fernando Alonso came fourth in the 2000 championship, winning one F3000 race. His outstanding performance at Spa propelled him, with the help of Adrian Campos and Flavio Briatore, into a Minardi seat for 2001.

1994 Michele & Martini

Michele Alboreto and Pier Luigi Martini made the most experienced line-up in Minardi history. The late, lamented Alboreto had been inherited from Scuderia Italia but he had known Minardi for years, scoring that F2 win in 1981. It was a homecoming for Michele at the very end of his Grand Prix career. He had soared with Ferrari in the 1980s but then tooled around in poor cars for five years. Like Graham Hill, he loved racing and saw no reason to follow the advice of friends by quitting.

"I drove for Ferrari and not long after I was driving for Minardi! I don't look just for the glamour, or to be at the top. I like to win, of course, but I have a passion for driving – I drive for pleasure and success, not for money."[1]

His swansong at Minardi was a good send off with some great qualifying laps and a point at Monaco which helped Minardi beat four other teams to tenth spot.

Aldo Costa, who was on his way out of Faenza, rates Alboreto, Martini and Fittipaldi as the best Minardi drivers he worked with. "I really enjoyed working with Michele as a driver but enjoyed also as a person, because he was always happy, smiling, transferring enthusiasm to the group. He had unbelievable style. Christian was very, very young and very, very motivated, and in '93 had some excellent races and we enjoyed that a lot. Both were good at feedback, very precise."

Minardi and Alboreto provided a relatively small footnote to the terrible weekend at Imola. A wheel came off in the pit lane and hospitalised four mechanics from Lotus and Ferrari.

It was unusual for Minardi to take older drivers in the autumn of their Grand Prix careers. Jos Verstappen and Ukyo Katayama would be the only others who, like Alboreto and Martini, would bow out at Minardi. Martini was unaccustomed to being the 'junior' partner but played a blinder in 1994 and twice finished fifth.

Minardi's long and complex relationship with Benetton team boss Flavio Briatore began in 1994. Gian Carlo Minardi secured a deal to run Mugen-Honda engines in '95 but the Japanese firm was persuaded to break the contract and move the engines to Briatore's new purchase Ligier. Minardi sued but was forced to back down when Briatore counter-sued and successfully impounded Minardi's equipment during the French GP at Ligier's base, Magny-Cours.

Michele's back! From left: Alboreto, Martini, Mariani Alessandro (race engineer), Minardi, Rene Hilhorst (aerodynamics), Renato Cappucci (sporting director), Gabriele Tredozi, Aldo Costa, Paolo Stanzani (managing director who came from Scuderia Italia). (Courtesy Giorgio Nada Editore)

Alboreto's problems at the San Marino Grand Prix were of minor significance. (Courtesy Giorgio Nada Editore)

Alboreto and Martini at the Imola launch. (Courtesy Giorgio Nada Editore)

"I claimed damages," explains Minardi. "Briatore played on the fact I hadn't paid a part of the engine supply. So there was this legal action, which ended in my favour. It was quite sensational that he had sequestrated everything. Much less sensational was that later I didn't pay the difference."

The failure to secure the engines was a hammer blow for technical director Aldo Costa, who was now planning to leave. "It was very bad because all of us believed that Minardi had a real chance. I went to Tokyo on my own, speaking with a lot of Japanese engineers, discussing in detail all the technical specifications of the engine, the power train in general, the cooling requirement. We had several meetings, they were pretty open because they told us, unofficially, that the deal was done. They were working really as part of our team. I was very impressed with the circulation of information especially with the time difference. Any day I sent a fax, coming back in the morning I received the answer and every day we did like that for a few weeks. All of a sudden, I sent a fax, the day after I didn't receive any answer, so I said 'oh, that's strange, the first time maybe it's a hiccup'. Then a second day, a third and then there was the announcement that Mugen was going to Ligier."

In 1995, Ligier/Mugen Honda would score 24 points and finish fifth. In 1996, Flavio Briatore would buy Minardi. Don't you love Formula 1?

At the end of '94, Luchinni was ready to sell up but would have to wait: the official entry for 1995 remained Minardi-Scuderia Italia.

[1] As said to Nigel Roebuck, archive quote used in *Motor Sport* magazine, October 2006.

1995

Bits & pieces

"We can't talk really about frustration," says Luca Badoer, sitting on a bench at Ferrari's pristine Fiorano test track. "Of course, I think it was better for me to get another opportunity maybe, for a medium or winning team, because I won everything in karting, F3 and F3000 and, for sure, I was able to win also in F1 but there is too much difference between the front and back – that's life!" he says with a latin shrug.

Luca became a key member of the Ferrari team that dominated Formula 1 at the beginning of the 21st century. Michael Schumacher frequently paid tribute to the Italian test driver who clocked up thousands of miles to help the Scuderia return to the big time. Back in 1995 though, as the 24-year-old Badoer replaced Alboreto at Faenza, he was a million miles away from Maranello in F1 terms, even if it was only 103km/64 miles in reality.

The good-looking M195 leads a less attractive Forti. Minardi only scored one point in the very last race. (Courtesy Giorgio Nada Editore)

"It was, of course, a very great experience," says Luca. "I have to say thank-you to Mr Minardi because he gave me two opportunities to drive in F1. He is a fantastic man and I am very sorry he is not involved anymore. The budgets meant we didn't have a very competitive team but, anyway, it was a very good experience both times."

Martini had stayed on for 1995 but it would be his last season at Minardi, a decade on from that troubled first year. '95 wasn't vastly better with one point at the very end and that scored by Martini's replacement.

Luca's best finishes would be a brace of eighths at Montreal and the Hungaroring while Martini finished just outside the points at Monaco and Silverstone. The next race at Hockenheim was Piero's last Grand Prix. He was demotivated, Minardi was skint and engine failure after 11 laps spelt the end. What a pity. Gian Carlo Minardi insists he doesn't get close to drivers; apart from one.

"From an affection point of view he is the exception, because he did 102 Grands Prix with us. Practically a third of Minardi history was written by Martini."[1]

Pier Luigi was 'the special one'. He was also Minardi's local hero, a fellow Romangnolo. "No doubt Piero paid dearly for his loyalty. Probably he could have done more. He also was lazy and late learning English. He was comfortable with the team, there was a lot of negativity which made him stay with us. At the end of 1989 when he had given Minardi the best technical and sporting results, he could have gone elsewhere."

They remain friends to this day. Like several frustrated Grand Prix drivers, a switch to sports cars would provide the success

Luca Badoer had a big one at Monza. (Courtesy Giorgio Nada Editore)

Piero so deserved. In 1999, he won the Le Mans 24 hours for BMW alongside Jo Winkelhock and Yannick Dalmas. GP racing wasn't out his system though and in April 2006 Piero joined the new Grand Prix Masters series, adding his great name to a grid which already included Mansell, Fittipaldi, Patrese, Arnoux, Warwick and even Minardi alumnus de Cesaris. Four races were planned for the first season' and Martini showed his pace early on in Qatar. Mind you, he was the youngest on the grid having reached the minimum age of 45 the previous weekend. Double world champion Emerson Fittipaldi is 14 years older but that hadn't prevented him harrying Nigel Mansell in the inaugural event at Kyalami in November 2005. Despite much scepticism, the South African race was a great success with more spectators than there'd been for the final F1 race in Johannesburg. The 600bhp GP Masters cars are marvellous according to the old racers and, predictably, Piero says far better than the last F1 car he drove.

Martini, now with a very good command of English, regrets he didn't speak it sooner. "It was my fault but there were some other drivers who didn't speak English, like Nakajima, who found good cars [but that was thanks to Honda]. The biggest problem for a racing team in Italy is the devotion to Ferrari. If you lose Ferrari you lose everything and that's not correct. It's not possible to be a second team in Italy. Minardi has a big passion inside of him and people understand that. He loves motor racing but in F1 you need big money. I stayed too long with Minardi but it was very difficult to find a good car. There were so many strong drivers – Mansell, Prost, Senna. I am happy about my history and every point at Minardi was a victory. In every other category I won and inside I am very happy. I was the best at Minardi! It's easy to win with a good car; more difficult to stay in front with a Minardi."

1995 also saw the departure of technical director Aldo Costa, who'd achieved about all he could on a shoestring budget. He confirms Minardi always made its lira go further than other teams. It was leaner, it worked smarter. "I have to say, coming here to Ferrari I was very pleased to find in Minardi for seven years we applied very, very good methodology, a very good system of work and we were very aggressive in a lot of development." Costa is particularly proud of the M189 (the first Costa/Cowperthwaite design) and the hydraulic suspension work for 1993-94.

"The comments were very good from the drivers, yes we had some problems," he laughs, "you have to imagine this, when Nigel left at the beginning of '90, the aerodynamic team was myself, Rene Hilhorst and Marco de Luca [in their first jobs], from there we were very methodical with the windtunnel.

"Obviously, we made mistakes like the front wings of the M192 and M195. We were learning all the aerodynamic behaviour and criteria on the car in the windtunnel and on the track – learning as we went. We discovered the stall characteristic of the cars, the aero mapping, steering effects, all these sort of things we were discovering by ourselves. Reliability was one of our strong points. Again, a good methodology I tried to bring here to Ferrari. It was not so nice here in 1995!"

Pedro Lamy stepped in to Martini's car. The 23-year-old Portuguese driver had broken both legs testing for Lotus but relaunched his career with Minardi, and it was he who scored the team's only point of 1995, at Adelaide's last Grand Prix.

Again, one point means so much. Tenth place in the championship ensured more money from the TV rights and free freight to the long-haul races. One of the teams Minardi beat, Pacific, failed to make the grid in 1996 and the other, Forti, was gone by the end of July. From 20 teams in 1989, the Formula 1 World Championship was down to 10.

It's fair to say motor racing attracts a particular sort of 'businessman'. One of Gian Carlo Minardi's mantras is about how he's always paid the bills, he always got by, that's why he had to keep the workforce small. By 1995, the bills were simply too much. The Minardi business model for Formula 1 was hopelessly outdated and this is when Flavio Briatore re-appears. Not that Gian Carlo saw him coming ...

"One morning at the Spanish Grand Prix, I went to the dad of all of us, Bernie Ecclestone and with my poor English I told him: "Bernie, I have these problems" and he replied: "Only that?" I said yes, only, but for me they are like a house weighing on my head, always speaking with my broken English. Bernie said "If these are your problems, don't worry". Of course, we were talking small numbers for Bernie. I looked at him half embarrassed and half happy, I think I didn't even say goodbye. I ran to get my nephew who was my assistant and I told him: "Renato, come with me, either I didn't understand a word or something is happening." We went back and Bernie said: "Don't worry, Monday morning you will get help." Monday morning at 10am Italian time, 9 in England, I got a call from the bank and they told me that I was about to receive X amount, what should we do? I said don't move and raced down there. In Montreal, I went into Bernie's office and there was Flavio Briatore. Together we quickly cancelled the company's debt."

Just like that. Here is the genius of Bernie Ecclestone, the man who knows where the bodies are buried. Along with Briatore he would arrange Paul Stoddart's 'purchase' of Minardi in 2001, bail out the Australian two years later (according to Stoddart) and in 2005 persuade Red Bull tycoon Dietrich Mateschitz, who already owned one team, to buy Minardi. Just keep the show on the road.

[1] Interview with *Autosport Atlas*, 2004

1996

Too many cooks

Money was tighter than Pedro Lamy's seatbelts at the start of the Australian Grand Prix. There was no way he could drive properly as he was thrown around the cockpit and Pedro soon crashed out. It typified Minardi's chaotic existence. Hapless Japanese rent-a-driver Taki Inoue was lined up for the second car until the deal fell apart at the last minute. Not for the first nor the last time, the ensuing legal action dragged on for years. With no Italian test driver it would have been Minardi's first ever season without an Italian in the squad. But as Taki took his leave, young Giancarlo Fisichella entered the frame with just days to spare. "Ten days before the race Minardi phoned me and said 'Get ready, because you're going to Australia,' and I said 'For what?' and he told me 'to race, you're going to be a Formula 1 driver.' I was really surprised!"

'Fisico' was a karting and Formula 3 prodigy and had tested for Minardi the previous year. He was the first of several Minardi 'trainees' who went on to great things in the late '90s and the new millennium. "The preparation wasn't so good because I didn't test enough but I was fit anyway. The race wasn't too bad, I was quicker than Lamy in qualifying. In the race I think I was around 11th or 12th, but after 32 laps I had a problem with hydraulics."

Safety measures post-Imola '94 demanded higher cockpits, yet cash-strapped Minardi was forced to adapt the existing car. It was also forced to run two more pay drivers in Giovanni Lavaggi (who failed to qualify at Hockenheim, Spa and Suzuka) and Tarso Marques (for the South American rounds).

"There are 37 drivers that have had the opportunity to drive in

Giancarlo Fisichella was handed the 1996 drive at the last minute. (Courtesy Giorgio Nada Editore)

Michael Schumacher, in his first season at Ferrari, prepares to lap the Minardi M195B of Pedro Lamy en route to a famous win at Spa. (Courtesy Giorgio Nada Editore)

F1 with us and we had the luck of working with them. They are all extremely important because when they raced with Minardi they helped us staying alive in every sense."[1]

Staying alive in 1996 required more than drivers. Fisico's eighth in Montreal was the high point, which pretty much says it all. These days, as he points out, it would have meant a point, yet this was the first of three seasons in which Minardi failed to trouble the scorers.

"All the guys were really, really enthusiastic," says Fisichella. "The atmosphere was just great. It was good to show my talent and, of course, it's where I met Flavio Briatore." Yes, the Benetton team manager, driver agent and all-round wheeler-dealer was back on the radar. He wasted little time in signing up Fisico and before loaning him to Jordan for 1997, had him test a Benetton.

Briatore led a consortium including Minardi old boy Sandro Nannini and Fondmetal wheels tycoon Gabriele Rumi; together they controlled 70 per cent of the stock. Apart from a minority shareholder, the remainder was divided equally between the rump of Scuderia Italia and Gian Carlo Minardi, who still ran the shop. He hoped in vain that Briatore could secure a supply of Mugen Hondas, but the Japanese opted to support their old friend Alain Prost as he embarked on team ownership. So Minardi spent a season away from its usual V8 Cosworths and had engines from Hart.

Nannini's driving career lay in the wreckage of a helicopter at his family's villa in 1990. For what it's worth, he had already told Maranello where to go with what he considered a poor offer for 1991:

"Ferrari were more interested with Alesi and selling road cars in France. I don't know why but then they offered an impossible contract and I said 'fuck off'."

An arm was successfully re-attached and in '96 Flavio got him back in an F1 car, testing for Benetton. The times were good but a fairy tale return to Minardi would have required extensive modifications to the car. Sandro now runs the family's baking and coffee business and will always have a special place in the hearts of

Minardi fans for his time in F2, his perseverance in the difficult early days of F1 and the fact he was one of the first Minardi 'graduates' to win a Grand Prix.

Briatore was busy building his stable of drivers – Fisichella's compatriot Jarno Trulli took the seat at Minardi. It was something Briatore appeared to enjoy, and in later years Fisico and Trulli would be shuffled around to the bemusement of them and everyone else. Flavio would shape Minardi's line-up for years to come.

Fisico is keen to pay tribute to his mentor and namesake: "I must say just thanks to Gian Carlo Minardi because he gave me the chance. He's a great man, with a big passion for F1 and what he did with his budget was just great. It's impossible to exist alongside Ferrari; it's impossible for Italian drivers too – even when Jarno and I get on the podium, it's still all about Ferrari." Fisico would, for years, angle for a berth at Maranello, but it never happened. The closest he got was driving for the Ferrari-powered Sauber team in 2004. Giancarlo hoped in vain that the odd test at Fiorano would lead to greater things. He always seemed to be in the right team at the wrong time and when he finally had a race-winning car, the Renault of 2005, he was thoroughly eclipsed by another Minardi graduate.

[1] *Autosport Atlas*, 2004

1997
Rumi to manoeuvre

Ukyo Katayama had already proved his worth in F1 when he brought his Mild Seven tobacco sponsorship to Minardi for a final year of GP racing. He retired halfway through the first race at Albert Park, but team-mate Jarno Trulli scored a solid ninth on his debut. A similar result in Argentina marked the high point for Minardi. Until Katayama, a Latin cast had filled the Minardi cockpits; Italians, of course, but also Spaniards, Brazilians and one Portuguese. From '97 onwards, Minardi would cast its net wider including an Australian, a Hungarian, three Dutchmen and even two Brits.

Jarno agrees with Paul Stoddart that it's far better for a young hotshot to start somewhere like Minardi, where expectations are naturally lower. Lewis Hamilton really is the exception who proves this rule; how many rookies are as well prepared, as cool, as the astonishing British protege? In common with the vast majority of gradutes of the 'University of Faenza', Trulli has good memories, "The team is like Gian Carlo's family. He treats everybody like a son and probably that was his mistake, if we can say there was one!"[1]

After Olivier Panis's bad crash at Montreal, Trulli switched to Prost and an upward trajectory. It allowed Tarso Marques to make the first of his Minardi comebacks at Magny-Cours. Another comeback, if only for one season, was a Minardi livery of yellow and blu notte. The colour schemes in the mid-nineties had reflected the turmoil in the team, but the M197 was a pleasant reminder.

It was an exceptional season in that Minardi was running Hart V8s. The hoped-for Mugen-Hondas propelled Prost to sixth place in the final table while the usual Cosworths ensured Stewart and Tyrrell finished ninth and tenth respectively. Minardi was once more off the chart.

British American Tobacco was actively seeking an entry to the championship and had its sights on Faenza. Briatore had no qualms about selling. Neither did his friend Nannini: "Rumi wanted to keep it Minardi so Briatore and I sold to him. He maybe made a mistake because it was a very big offer."

BAT then focussed on a team of faded glory based near Guildford in England. Ken Tyrrell agreed to stay on as figurehead during the transitional year of 1998 but soon resigned in disgust at the makeweight drivers who were forced upon him. "More money than sense" was the paddock consensus in 1999 on British American Racing, as Jacques Villeneuve and his manager Craig

Ukyo Katayama and the M197 at Imola. (Courtesy Giorgio Nada Editore)

Jarno Trulli raced for Minardi just six times.
(Courtesy Giorgio Nada Editore)

Pollock tried and failed to build a winning team. After a number of upheavals that team became Honda for 2006 and has only once troubled the podium's top step at time of writing. Ironically, BAT's purchase of Tyrrell foiled a certain Paul Stoddart.

"Absolutely, there were quite a few twists in all of this," says the Australian. "I actually gave Bob Tyrrell a deposit cheque for US$5m. He sat and held it in his hand for a good hour over a couple of glasses of wine. Finally, he tore it up and gave it back to me and I've still got it in my office drawer to this day. He said 'I just can't do it, I just can't do it, I've committed to BAT.'" A near miss for the aviation tycoon, but he was determined to get into F1.

Within three years, Paul Stoddart would own Minardi and be working with its stalwart designer Gabriele Tredozi. He's a huge part of the Minardi story; a loyal lieutenant who was there at the end, he was almost there at the beginning and he designed the M197. But 1998 would see the return of Gustav Brunner and Nigel Cowperthwaite as Rumi, to his eternal credit, ploughed money into Minardi. An old friend from Maranello, Cesare Fiorio, was brought in as sporting director. The three-year plan included strengthening both the human and technical assets in 1998, to produce better results in '99 and then become a strong midfield team in 2000, challenging the likes of Benetton, Sauber and Jordan. Minardi and Rumi would form a close bond over the next three seasons as Faenza made its final, concerted push for glory.

[1] *Autosport* 31.3.2005

Minardi's owners: Nannini, Pallanzani o Pallazzani, Rumi, Briatore and Minardi.
(Courtesy Giorgio Nada Editore)

1998

Much too young

It was sink or swim for Gabriele Rumi. His Fondmetal team of the early '90s had failed, and he now found himself holding someone else's baby. The partnership with Gian Carlo Minardi was fruitful; Rumi making the big calls, Minardi running the team day-to-day. A quite different arrangement to the Stoddart years, but frankly, where else could a team founder have such an input so long after losing financial control? Neither Rumi nor Stoddart changed the name over the door, as was their right. Minardi admits Rumi felt isolated by the departure of Briatore and others: "He felt a little bit abandoned by everyone.[1]

"Those years were really intense. I was a shareholder. It was really difficult during those years, there were 12 or 13 teams, the key was to stay within the first ten in order to benefit from TV rights which were increasing year after year, so you always had to do better."

Money came in courtesy of Shinji Nakano, a second Japanese driver who'd scored points at Prost, and Argentine Esteban Tuero. At 19 years 10 months and 14 days, Tuero was then the third youngest driver to make a Grand Prix grid, and, unlike Fernando Alonso in 2001, arrived in the top flight far too soon. He came in eighth at Imola and Nakano had a seventh in Montreal. The only team to do worse in 1998 was an entry which was Tyrrell in name only.

Minardi's cars were a striking silver and blue and Gustav Brunner was hard at work on the design for 1999, the M01. He'd started at ATS in the 1970s, worked at Ferrari and masterminded Minardi's successful '93 car before returning to Maranello. The enigmatic Austrian would make a dramatic exit of his own in 2001 but in 1998 it was a driver. Minardi says one of his biggest shocks in F1 was Esteban Tuero's bizarre decision to walk out on the team on the eve of the next season. "We were just left with our jaws dropped. He quit and just left. We didn't even notice his taxi was waiting outside."[2]

One suspects the team missed the cash rather more than the man. Young Spaniard Marc Gene had won a winter test with Minardi at Barcelona, and after finding sponsorship from Telefonica was drafted swiftly.

[1] *Autosport Atlas*, 2004

1999 Raindance

It had been more than two years since Luca Badoer had last driven in a Grand Prix for Forti. Since then he'd been testing for the resurgent Scuderia Ferrari. However, racing drivers need to race and Luca was back, albeit on the understanding that he was Maranello's reserve driver. On the grid at Albert Park he must have wondered why he wanted to be back at Minardi; the only man he'd out-qualified was rookie team-mate Marc Gene. Badoer had taken the place of Nakano at the eleventh hour; the money men behind the young Japanese failed to deliver. Prost tester Stephane Sarrazin subbed for an injured Badoer at round two in Brazil. He out-qualified four other cars including that of his team-mate Gene but it was to be the Frenchman's first and last Grand Prix, ending with wing failure and a big crash. Uniquely versatile in the modern era, Sarrazin went on to score impressive results in sports and rally cars. He finished runner-up at Le Mans 2007, sharing his Peugeot with former Minardi man Pedro Lamy [Gene would finish fourth].

Minardi's technical package for 1999 was much improved and the team worked hard to out-qualify Arrows. At the home race at Imola, Badoer came in eighth followed by Gene. Luca thought his big break had come at Silverstone when Michael Schumacher suffered a big break of his own; in his leg. Halfway through the first lap, Luca sped past Schumacher's wreckage at Stowe. But the call from Maranello did not come. Instead, Mika Salo, a proven points scorer who had been subbing successfully at BAR, was to partner Eddie Irvine. The Finn surrendered certain victory to Irvine at Hockenheim, both lapping Badoer in the process. It was a shattering blow for the luckless Italian. "Yeah, I was expecting a call but they already had other plans and I was involved with Minardi so ... I'm not the right person to answer this question," he smiles. Who is? "Maybe Jean Todt can give you exactly the right answer!"

Several requests were made to the Maranello press office. The Ferrari F1 boss declined the opportunity to comment.

Luca doesn't seem too bothered about it now. The Italian driver lives and breathes Scuderia Ferrari, bringing his children to Fiorano and hanging out in Enzo's house. He's driven some of the best cars ever created but there must be a niggle somewhere about 1999, about what might have been.

Could things get worse? Well, yes. The European Grand Prix at the Nürburgring threw one of those curve balls which occasionally confound the big teams. Fortunately, Minardi had age and guile on the pit wall. It also had some fine drivers who were able to

Luca who's back for more.
(Courtesy Giorgio Nada Editore)

show what they could do thanks to rain; wet races always level the technical playing field and driver skill becomes far more apparent. The rain started on lap 17 and as Häkkinen and Irvine suffered pit stop nightmares, both Coulthard and Fisichella threw away the lead.

With thirteen laps to go, Luca Badoer was running fourth when the gearbox went. Poor Luca crumpled behind the armco barrier. Here's Gian Carlo Minardi. "A perfect race very well managed by Fiorio, myself and Gabriele Tredozi. We made some outstanding tyre changes. Herbert won the race for Stewart and when we withdrew we were in front of him. With Badoer we could have been among the top three, which is what Minardi is missing. It was a beautiful race and at the end Gene's points earned us the tenth placing [for the season]. On one hand we were happy; on the other we were sad knowing we had missed a great opportunity." It was ten years on from the deluge in Adelaide.

Luca has a different memory of the pit stops. He thinks he should have been running even higher. "Unfortunately, we had a problem with the gearbox seven or eight laps from the end. The car was fantastic because we had raining, dry, raining, dry – I did all the race on dry tyres and this was very good. I was fourth and, I have to say, with the wrong pit stop, otherwise it would have been an even better result. Then I had the gearbox problem. I was really very sad because, for me and Minardi, fourth position was really fantastic."

Gabriele Rumi: "His lap times were unbelievable, among the fastest and he, therefore, deserved really much more. His retirement, on such a favourable day, ruins a little joy a bit."

The joy was a point for Marc Gene: "I am very happy for the team because this is the result of a whole year's work. The car was

Big sponsorship was still a struggle for one of the most stylish Minardis.
(Courtesy Giorgio Nada Editore)

Opposite: Marc Gene and the M01 at Monaco.
(Courtesy Giorgio Nada Editore)

very good. Gustav Brunner and the technical staff made a very competitive car. Today Fiorio's strategy proved excellent. Also my engineers did an extraordinary job setting up the car in the best way. I, therefore, feel truly satisfied especially for the team. They have been waiting for this outcome for a long time. They all did an extraordinary job."

Luca and Marc would team up once more as Ferrari's test drivers in 2005, Luca by then a long-time servant of Maranello. Michael Schumacher doesn't doubt the input from the former Minardi man, and they have formed a good friendship. It made this writer's day to see the two sharing a joke outside Enzo Ferrari's house, on the edge of the Fiorano circuit the Old Man had marked out in the early 1970s.

Very few Grand Prix careers do not finish in failure, but the epitaph for Luca is cruel, soothed only by the knowledge he beat Rubens Barrichello to the 1992 F3000 title and the fact he's developed some of the best racing cars in history. However, Luca Badoer holds a record which may never be broken: 49 GP starts without a single point.

2000

New millennium, old story

A Minardi trademark, alongside talent-spotting and great coffee, is a stylish paint job. The toxic yellow confection for 2000 is not one of them. It was due to more sponsorship from Spanish telecom giant Telefonica, as Gabriele Rumi looked to Marc Gene's homeland for more cash. There was even talk of moving Minardi to Barcelona along with a buy-out by the South American broadcaster PSN. The latter accounted for Argentine make-weight Gaston Mazzacane to partner Gene, now in his second year at Minardi.

The Cosworth V10 was in its third year and probably ready for an historic racing series rather than the Formula 1 World Championship, but that didn't prevent Minardi making big progress. The M02 was one of Gustav Brunner's best designs and it gained two seconds to the big teams, a stunning achievement when one considers the engines involved and the relative budgets.

"If a manufacturer finishes last in the championship, it's very unlikely they'll continue in F1," says Marc Gene. "I think private teams need to be there because they are the only ones who can afford not to be very successful sometimes with results. A top manufacturer can't afford that. Teams like Minardi were the only ones who nurtured new talent, top manufacturers cannot afford that. I have a lot of respect and I am really thankful to Minardi because they gave me the chance, I learnt a lot with them. It's a really, really sad thing for everybody that Minardi isn't there anymore."

There were no points in 2000, so highlights were Minardi's 250th GP at Spa and reigning champion Mika Hakkinen trying in vain to pass Mazzacane at Indianapolis. Boosted by this, the Argentine driver took his PSN sponsorship to Prost and career oblivion. It was a strange thing to do as Minardi had beaten Prost in the championship operating on $60m, less than half the budget available to the French.[1]

When Telefonica then withdrew the Barcelona relocation plan, it was the end of the road for the Rumi/Minardi axis, not least because Rumi was gravely ill. "Our only option was to donate, that's the right word, everything to Paul Stoddart, who in turn took on all the company's debt," says Minardi. "I think Stoddart's biggest stroke of luck was to be in a ten team World Championship. He reduced research and management expenses to a minimum; we raced three years with the same monocoque. He stuck it out until he had a once in a lifetime opportunity and he took advantage of it."

"That's absolutely true," says Stoddart. "Minardi didn't have the money to fund the development that was needed to be in the top ten."

Bernie Ecclestone, well versed in Faenza's hand-to-mouth existence, selected Stoddart to take the 'franchise'. "Yes," laughs Ecclestone, "he scraped in. Completely different way of operating to Gian Carlo. We all know what Paul was, we all know exactly what the difference between him and Gian Carlo was. We had an awful lot of trouble with Stoddart and we had none with Gian Carlo. It would have gone out of business anyway if he hadn't bought. It's one of those things that had to happen."

Paul Stoddart loves a deal as much as he loves racing. The Australian tycoon says he paid $50m for the team and another $30m to fund the losses.

Stoddart was now in total charge, the 'Padre Padrone', literally the father and master. He could have changed the name, he could have closed the factory in Faenza and moved everything to the UK, yet he didn't. The prohibitive cost was the main reason, but Stoddart and his technical team were also very impressed by what they

Money talks, bullshit walks. Telefonica title sponsorship in 2000 would not last. (Courtesy Giorgio Nada Editore)

found in Italy. Like Rumi, Stoddart chose to not only keep the name, tradition and staff of Minardi, but to keep the man as well. Gian Carlo would later joke he did “everything and nothing” at Faenza. Despite losing all his shares, he still had a seat on the board and would advise Paul but only when asked. It was a rather odd arrangement with inevitable tensions. Over the final seasons, Gian Carlo would continue as the day-to-day figurehead at the factory, opening it up each morning. He busied himself with co-ordinating things, talent-spotting, helping find sponsorship, advising on race weekends. Paul Stoddart says he has no regrets in keeping Minardi involved and, anyway, the person really running the team day-to-day was John Walton.

Gian Carlo and Paul agree on how the Australian lucked out, or thought he had, with his timing. German media giant Kirch had just invested $2 billion in Formula 1 and wasn’t going to let anything jeopardise it, certainly nothing as trifling as grid numbers. If small teams needed help, they would get it. As soon as grids were down to 20 cars in 2002, Stoddart had various people over a barrel.

Was he just waiting for a time to cash in his chips or did he really want Minardi to improve? Of course, he wanted it to improve – but if it couldn’t ...

[1] *The Piranha Club* (page 300), Timothy Collings

2001

I come from a land down under

"When I came in it was dead. There were people literally walking out of the door." Paul Stoddart.

Latin blood had coursed through Minardi F1 for 16 years, but the ill health of Gabriele Rumi changed all that. Things were about to get Anglo-Saxon, in more ways than one. Wheeler-dealing is in the DNA of every team principal so Paul Stoddart was going to fit right in. Making his fortune in air charter, freight and spares, the Australian had based his European Aviation empire in the UK. At the start of the year he had no idea 2001 was precisely the wrong time to enter Formula 1. September 11th and a less stable world were still unimaginable.

Stoddart had been hovering around F1 for a while as a sponsor, taking the pit board duties at Tyrrell and buying the stock when the end came for Ken. Ironically, his earlier bid to buy the Tyrrell team was indirectly frustrated by Rumi and Minardi. They had refused, in 1997, to sell out to a British American Tobacco consortium which then purchased Tyrrell. It made Stoddart more determined to get into Formula 1. He tried in vain to buy into Jordan (at its zenith in 1999) and later to buy Arrows (until his accountants told him to walk away). With former staff of Tyrrell and Honda Racing Developments, Stoddart had been running an F3000 team and building his corporate two-seater F1 business, all the time watching for openings in the world of one-seaters.

"I'd been following the PSN episode with Minardi. The interesting thing was we were always close to the to-ings and fro-ings because Minardi used to occupy the garage next to Tyrrell

or next to Arrows," laughs Stoddart. "I also had good friends at Cosworth who said the engine situation was pretty hopeless; we then heard Renault/Supertec had come in and made a bid. Obviously, [my friend] Mike Gascoyne was now working at Renault. I was talking to him and Flavio and so was aware when they pulled out. Mike rang me and said 'if you want to buy this, get on a plane and go now because we're out of it.' I had a quick meeting with Flavio and Bruno Michel of Renault, who'd been very involved in the due diligence of Minardi. They were so close to death I was very lucky Flavio and Bruno were kind enough to tell me a quick version of what they'd found. It was then a commercial decision from me as to whether I wanted to do it or not. I flew over there on the 9th of January 2001 and, as they say, the rest is history.

"Rumi knew he had cancer and, understandably, he was passionate about motor racing, he'd put a lot of money in to keep Minardi alive and he'd lost a lot of money. It's fair to say once he was diagnosed with cancer he wanted it to go to a new home. It was one less burden he had to worry about, that his family had to worry about. By the time I took it over it was very risky, to say the least, and we were several million in before we even had a heads of agreement. There was an immense amount of debt. US$22.9m [basic] was what I paid for the team and by the end of 2001 it owed me a significant amount more than that. We assumed the debt, we paid Rumi and enormous amounts of creditors and also the costs of funding and running the team. Not to be forgotten is the fact we had to do our own engine supply, which was no mean feat."

"I've always had faith," says Gian Carlo. "There's always been the song 'Minardi disappears'; I've always been convinced that Minardi was here to stay. Indeed, later Minardi stopped because it was sold to someone who kept the structure alive. The name has changed and this happens when someone buys, but Minardi's foundation has not been lost. In any case, at that point I wasn't a shareholder."

Stoddart had just six weeks and three days to get two cars on the grid for the first race of the season in, of all places, his hometown Melbourne. It was a remarkable achievement by all concerned and he rates it as his greatest.

The PS01 was launched on steps of the state Parliament of Victoria; politicians adjourned so they could be part of the F1 action.

The previous few weeks had been anything but glamorous. Hot-desking is common in offices but Stoddart invented 'hot-bedding' for his staff and it's far from romantic. They were working around the clock to build the cars, and 30 staff from the UK were also drafted in. Minardi commandeered its local hotel, the Cavallino, so when one person was so exhausted they couldn't go on at the factory, they would kick someone else out of bed to replace them.

Former Tyrrell fabricator Eddie Marrian was one of the British staff despatched to Italy. "I was used to winter builds at Tyrrell and it was a lot of hard work, so when Paul walked down the stairs and said 'I've bought a Formula 1 team' a lot of people were happy but I knew what it meant," he laughs. It was daunting walking into Faenza but everyone simply had to knuckle down together. "It was only when you could show that you could actually make things, that you were an ordinary working Joe like them, that they sort of calmed

As easy as riding a bike: Gian Carlo Minardi (right) puts Paul Stoddart in the saddle.
(Courtesy Sutton Motorsport Images)

Back to black; the PS01 made it to the grid by a matter of hours. (Courtesy Sutton Motorsport Images)

down a bit. They were very paranoid and there were lots of stories going around about how maybe Paul was going to close down Faenza and bring it all to England. I think when he saw how good they were and what they were doing with what they had, it was best to just leave it there."

With the deadline looming, some humble engine brackets, manufactured in Sheffield, almost foiled the operation. Stoddart had to get one of his pilots to fetch the parts in the middle of the night but thick fog in Italy made returning impossible: or so he thought. The new team boss couldn't even see the fence at Forli airport and phoned the pilot at Coventry telling him not to bother. The pilot, who Stoddart only refers to as 'Nick', told him it would be fine before turning off his phone and taking off from England. He successfully landed in Italy, delivering his small titanium cargo to Stoddart. "I couldn't see anything at Forli. I asked him how much visibility he had but we never spoke about it. I'm told he had enough but perhaps I have private thoughts about that."

They were still flat out at the factory. "We'd just go to sleep, wake up, get straight in and you'd work until you needed to go to sleep again," says Eddie Marrian. "We had a lorry waiting to go to the airport and we were still welding radiators and pressure testing them. We were just getting as many bits as we could onto that lorry as possible, it was murder. We didn't have any spares so if there had been problems in qualifying that would have been it."

Paul Stoddart: "[After the race at Melbourne] I came off the pit wall and I walked back in and I was really happy because Fernando had got 12th place. No Formula 1 car in history has had less running than that one before it raced. Tarso's car was built in the garage and Fernando had just one 50km shakedown at Fiorano, that was it. He made me very proud, I was elated and when I got to

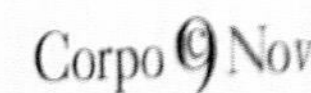

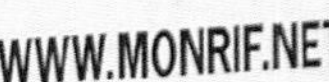

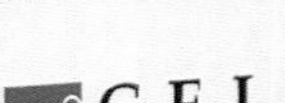

A star is born. Fernando Alonso in his first season of Grand Prix racing. (Courtesy Sutton Motorsport Images)

The hills are alive with the sound of Minardi. (Courtesy Sutton Motorsport Images)

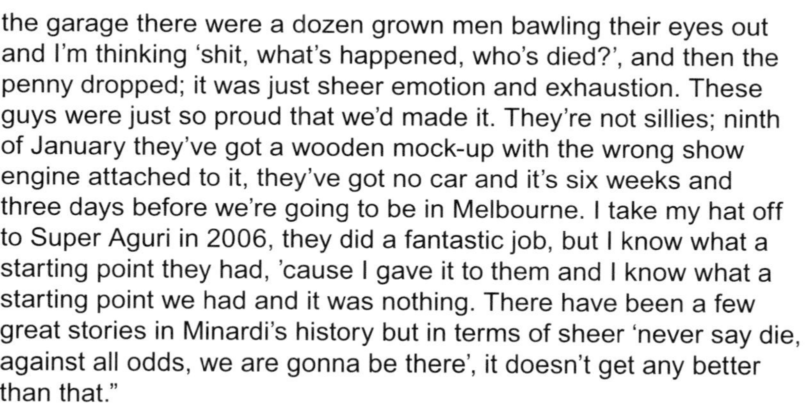

the garage there were a dozen grown men bawling their eyes out and I'm thinking 'shit, what's happened, who's died?', and then the penny dropped; it was just sheer emotion and exhaustion. These guys were just so proud that we'd made it. They're not sillies; ninth of January they've got a wooden mock-up with the wrong show engine attached to it, they've got no car and it's six weeks and three days before we're going to be in Melbourne. I take my hat off to Super Aguri in 2006, they did a fantastic job, but I know what a starting point they had, 'cause I gave it to them and I know what a starting point we had and it was nothing. There have been a few great stories in Minardi's history but in terms of sheer 'never say die, against all odds, we are gonna be there', it doesn't get any better than that."

Fernando Alonso came courtesy of his managers, one-time Minardi driver Adrian Campos and former team owner Flavio Briatore. The 19-year-old Spaniard had been wowing Formula 3000 and Flavio saw Minardi as the proving ground before a probable Benetton/Renault drive. In a season which saw the debuts of Räikkönen and Montoya, Alonso had to be a bit special to get noticed. He was.

In Melbourne, he qualified 19th and finished 12th. In the fourth race at Imola, he outqualified both Benettons, a Prost and his team-mate. That certainly got the attention of Pat Symonds at Benetton who, four years later, marshalled Fernando's campaign for the World Championship.

"Yes, it was good," laughs Alonso at the memory of being watched by his future boss. "We didn't have the worst car, we were fighting with the Prosts, with Arrows, so we had some good fighting."

Autosport's F1 guru Mark Hughes believes Fernando is Michael Schumacher's true heir, and he has done so since that weekend at Imola. "I particularly recall bumping into Gustav Brunner [Minardi technical director] shortly after qualifying. I commented that he looked a bit shell-shocked. 'Yes, I know the aero figures of this car, I know the power figures, the torque and power curves. But I don't know how those figures could possibly translate into the lap time that car has just done. I can only believe that it must be the driver – he must be doing things beyond what nearly all the other drivers are doing.'"[1]

The year of the September 11th attacks was exactly the wrong time for an aviation tycoon to buy an F1 team. (Courtesy Sutton Motorsport Images)

Adrian Campos, Fernando Alonso, Alonso Snr and Paul Stoddart. (Courtesy Sutton Motorsport Images)

"Suzuka was special," says Paul Stoddart, "and you have to have been in the team to know. Fernando had a lot of good performances that year but the one that stands out undoubtedly for me is Suzuka. On the Saturday afternoon he's qualified, we now know he's going to do a year of testing [for Renault], there was a lot of argument about that, so it's his last race and, quite traditionally, on the Sunday morning warm-up you used to let your driver go out for a 'glory lap', light on fuel. Somehow, he hadn't done that lap and there'd been a bit of a dispute between the two engineers so he went out with a proper fuel load. Fernando was clearly uptight and upset by this and,

"We didn't have the worst car, we were fighting with the Prosts, with Arrows." Fernando Alonso. (Courtesy Sutton Motorsport Images)

in true professional attitude, all we did was just demonstrate to the team, the engineers and the world at large just how good he was because if anyone looks at the lap times in the race he performed 53 qualifying laps. The only difference was either traffic, degradation in his tyres or the lessening in his fuel load. It is an unbelievable performance and in my mind the most outstanding race he's ever done."

Fernando: "It was the last race and I finished 11th in front of six cars because seventeen finished the race. I remember I lapped Panis in the BAR; it was the first time I lapped someone with the Minardi. I was proud of that one." Who would have thought? Fernando even learned how to lap people while at Minardi. Suzuka was a great send-off because he had quality finishing behind him. His 'best' result was actually scored at Hockenheim when he finished tenth but it was a race of high attrition, Fernando the last of the finishers. The decision to send him to Minardi, by his mentors Campos and Briatore, taught him patience. Fernando appreciates it now and insists he appreciated it at the time despite qualifying near the back for the first time in his short career.

"I think it's always nice to race, you get experience racing, not testing. 2001 was very important for me, it was my debut in F1 with not much expectations because in Minardi you never get any results. It was time for me to learn and to grow up in F1 and it was a really, really positive year for me, for my career, I believe."

As a 25-year-old double world champion, Fernando took his number one status to McLaren for 2007, alongside rookie Lewis Hamilton. I asked Fernando about the expectations on the young Brit and the difference between starting out at Minardi and McLaren.

"My expectation was simply to finish races because I only finished five in 2001, [the Minardi] was breaking up always."

Alonso says the final race in Suzuka was his best. Stoddart describes it as "53 qualifying laps." (Courtesy Sutton Motorsport Images)

"He must be doing things beyond what nearly all the other drivers are doing." Gustav Brunner. (Courtesy Sutton Motorsport Images)

Would he have preferred to start at a big team?

"I don't know, it's difficult. If you start at a small team you have no pressure and you learn things slowly and it's good, but if you start in a big team you have a lot of pressure and you have a lot of things to do apart from driving the car like media, like pressure. It's true that in the big teams you get the results; in a way it's good [for Lewis]." It's fair to say Hamilton made an impression on his debut.

Alonso is not arrogant. Nor is he falsely modest. He simply states he thought he was the quickest driver on the grid from day one. An expression of 'The Right Stuff' if ever one there was. Wasn't Adrian Campos worried his young compatriot would suffer, as he had at Faenza?

"Drivers have to take chances and look ahead. The only possibility was Minardi but my decision was it was his opportunity afterwards with Renault – 13 years later it was him and not me! I knew all the people, I knew many people who can help and it was completely different for Fernando. [Now] it's fantastic to see a

Spanish driver in a good car – it was my obsession. Minardi was a great first year. I demonstrated to the Spanish people they could have a world champion. I told journalists here that the moment we have a champion it'll be the same as Real Madrid and Barcelona together and that's what has happened."

After opening an early lead in the 2005 championship, Fernando's campaign was one of remarkable maturity. He calmly resisted Schumacher at Imola and was assured as he played the percentages in the second half of the season. When it stayed in one piece, Kimi Räikkönen's McLaren was surely quicker at many races, yet Alonso kept it together. Flavio Briatore suspected what he had after Alonso's F3000 win in 2000, and knew what he had after the apprenticeship at Minardi in 2001: another Michael Schumacher. And maybe, just maybe, more. "Everyone now recognises I made the right move [replacing Jenson Button with Alonso at the end of 2002]. I like Jenson, and for sure he's a very good driver, but I didn't see a long-term future with him. I built up Benetton with Michael and I wanted to do the same at Renault with Fernando. If the system works, why change it?"[2]

Faenza had helped toughen up Alonso; not in a nasty way but, as he says, in terms of maturity. If there is a set-back at the track, Alonso doesn't stew over it. Here's *Autosport* sage Nigel Roebuck writing at the time of Alonso's championship success: "Fernando's serenity is good-humoured and easy [unlike Räikkönen]. He

Both cars would retire at Monaco.
(Courtesy Sutton Motorsport Images)

Monaco: a sunny place for shady people.
(Courtesy Sutton Motorsport Images)

Fernando kerbs his enthusiasm in Montreal. Tarso qualified quicker. (Courtesy Sutton Motorsport Images)

Alonso qualified 18th out of 22 at Monaco. Gearbox failure put him out of the race. (Courtesy Sutton Motorsport Images)

exudes quiet confidence like no-one I have seen in this era, save Schumacher in his pomp ... Alonso can be a streetfighter if necessary, as everyone from Schumacher down knows, but more usually, in the way he coolly and methodically tackles a grand prix weekend, he reminds one of Alain Prost, whose every thought was always focussed on Sunday afternoon, when the points are paid out." Fernando would beat Juan Pablo Montoya and Kimi Raikkonen, his fellow 2001 debutants, to the world championship but came unstuck in 2007 with the seismic debut of Lewis Hamilton. The very self-belief that propelled him to such heights was counter-productive as he tried to deal with the rookie in identical equipment. Fernando would leave McLaren after just one season.

As with most Minardi graduates, Fernando looks back on his time at Faenza with great fondness.

"Paul Stoddart arrived in 2001, we always had some funny times on his planes, with all the mechanics before and after the races. I remember that time with a smile on my face. Paul was a funny guy, passionate about motor racing. He forgot any strategy, any tyres, any engine, he only focussed on the show for people and to get the drivers happy, to get the mechanics happy, the ambience was really different to other teams. Paul gave this atmosphere, there was no pressure for results, he only wanted to enjoy motor racing and all the team was enjoying the racing, even if we finished last."

His spell at Minardi shows the way to go for any promising young driver. With a few notable exceptions, it's far better to start at a small team with low expectations, than to arrive in a blizzard of hype (see Button and Montoya).

Fernando Alonso is the youngest ever race winner, the youngest ever world champion, the first Spanish world champion and the first Minardi graduate to become world champion. Surely, Gian Carlo, the best Minardi driver ever?

"I think it's fair to say that he's the best pilot today. Alonso has been a key pilot for the Minardi team, I'm happy he has reached

A Spaniard drives for Italian-Australian team in French Canada. (Courtesy Sutton Motorsport Images)

Money was always a problem; dedication was not. Minardi mechanics work the night away. (Courtesy Sutton Motorsport Images)

the results that I have somewhat predicted, but all Minardi pilots have been key players. Thanks to all of them it's been possible to race for 21 years and 340 Grand Prix. We've had many talented people. At Monza 2003 40 per cent of the drivers either had made their debut or raced with Minardi. Even in 2006 there were five former Minardi pilots. Who manages to stay at these levels is a talented person. For me they are all equal."

Well, maybe not all of them. In Alonso's considerable shadow was his team-mate Tarso Marques. Paul smiles as he recalls the likeable Brazilian. "Tarso paid me $15,000 for that drive! I always got on with him. He was in the right place at the right time and promised me deals. Him and Fernando got on fantastic, it all worked but the sponsorship never came. I think that was the cheapest ever F1 drive!"

It wasn't all smiles. The paddock piranhas hadn't waited long for their first bite of Paul Stoddart. Minardi's acclaimed technical director Gustav Brunner was lured by the prospects of Toyota F1 and informed Stoddart by hand-written fax in early May. "Paul, sorry. I do not have good news for you. I have signed with Toyota and I start with them tomorrow. The 2002 car, as you know, is designed. Sorry. Gustav."

Gabriele Tredozi once more took control of the design office at Faenza, as Stoddart called for the contracts recognition board to widen its jurisdiction from drivers to also cover senior staff. Minardi says they were all stunned; "One Friday night he left and in his Italian-German said 'I'm going home to cut the lawn' and he never returned. It wasn't a good moment for us. The Minardi team has always been a team, not a bunch of single players; today we have 70-80 people in key positions in other teams, including the top teams. Brunner was like a lighthouse, he was able to reassure whoever was around him. He had a lot of experience, based on his years at Ferrari. We couldn't afford to lose him. Toyota offered him four times what we were able to offer, which was already for us a lot of money. He was a great database."

Tarso Marques in unfamiliar territory; leading Alonso in Malaysia. (Courtesy Sutton Motorsport Images)

In 2000, Alonso had wowed Spa in F3000. A year later he was back in a Formula 1 car. (Courtesy Sutton Motorsport Images)

Aldo Costa knew Brunner better than most after the Austrian's first stint at Faenza. "Gustav is Gustav, he is like that. He's a very bright guy, a very honest guy, but he wants to take decisions immediately, so for him if he worked for a team his commitment is 100 per cent, but then if he's not feeling good anymore he will just leave, and he did; I worked with him very, very well but he has some strange behaviour."

Paul Stoddart blew the first of many gaskets over that betrayal, but he ended 2001 dreaming of a podium. He wouldn't have to wait long.

[1] *Autosport* 11.1.2007
[2] *Autosport* 6.4.2006

2002

Much too Yoong

"I've always said Formula 1 isn't a finishing school, so when you arrive you're saying you're ready," says Mark Webber when asked about Alex Yoong. "It's every man for himself and that's the way it's always been."

The inexperienced Anglo-Malaysian wasn't saying 'I'm ready' as much as 'here are the readies', to the tune of $11m. He and his father amazed themselves at how much they raised in such a short time but it was now or never. Alex admits it was a mistake. "Like all drivers, Formula 1 was a dream come true but it didn't go the way I wanted it to. I'm quite OK with it now but at the time it was very hard for me. I really wasn't quite ready for F1. I'd been in Japan doing Formula Nippon for a year and a half and it was very, very tough going. We had no money, I had a couple of accidents, very low confidence in my driving at the time, I just wasn't driving well. My career was about to stop. We always kind of knew it was going to happen, but Minardi offered me a test and I suddenly got all this attention back home in Malaysia and we suddenly raised a lot of money. My father, my manager and I discussed 'should we do it?', I was very apprehensive because my results weren't very good but the fact of the matter was if I didn't do Formula 1 I would have to stop racing."

The 2002 cars had a distinctive yellow 'Go KL' on the sidepods (Go Kuala Lumpur) and an improved engine deal with Asiatech. Malaysia had an F1 circuit and now had its own driver; local expectations were sky high, too high, but the result in the opening race in Melbourne did nothing to check them.

Alonso had swapped places with Renault's Australian tester Mark Webber, who had an unforgettable F1 debut in his homeland.

The deal was sealed in a Bernie-sort-of-way by one of Bernie's closest allies, Ron Walker. A bigwig in Australia's Liberal Party, he'd been responsible for Melbourne's controversial and successful bid to move the Grand Prix from Adelaide. With a Melbourne man now running an F1 team, Albert Park was guaranteed a record crowd if it had an Aussie driver. "The Australian contingent knew all about Paul and what he was trying to do to Formula 1," says Walker. "He was brash, he was courageous, he was focussed and he was determined and Bernie got on very well with him. We kept throwing out the images of Paul and Mark and the car on the TV [in the days before the race], it was great. It was all about them in the media and I'm sure Michael Schumacher and the others felt it."

Paul Stoddart, Mark Webber and Ron Walker appear on Australian TV from a late night London TV studio. (Courtesy Sutton Motorsport Images)

He says most Australian fans, despite their dominance in other sports, enjoyed cheering for the underdogs. "It was the way we marketed Paul; the man from Coburg [a Melbourne suburb] who grew up with nothing and made good through the world of aviation. That was the image we were selling rather than the Minardi car because that brand name meant nothing here. The battling underdog worked a treat because there were celebrations at Parliament House, the premier of the state of Victoria gave him a reception and we were able to build the image of Paul; a young man made good on the international scene coming back to his hometown."

"It was the most emotional weekend I've ever had," says Stoddart. "You've got to remember, I'm born and bred in Melbourne, I'm coming home to a hero's welcome, in my own 747, our first ever 747 flight, you've got the cars on board, you've got the drivers, the team ... I thought 'it just doesn't get any better than this' but it just kept getting better.

"Qualifying still had the dreaded 107% rule and I thought 'I know Mark's going to make it but all the backing's coming from Alex and Malaysia, shit, how stupid are we going to look if he doesn't qualify?' Halfway through qualifying it started to rain quite heavily and the commentator came to me and said 'I suppose you want it to dry up so you can have another crack at it?'. I said 'Hell no, I want it to absolutely piss down'. I forgot I had the microphone in my hand 'come on you lot get up and do a rain dance'. I was just messing around but the stands opposite did stand up and do a rain dance and it bucketed down and that was the end of qualifying so Alex got in."

On race day there was carnage at the first corner. Ralf Schumacher hit the back of Rubens Barrichello's Ferrari and sailed over him. It set off a chain reaction but the two Minardis were looking good. That advantage would have meant nothing if there had been a re-start but, amazingly, track marshals manhandled some of the eight stricken cars out of harm's way. It meant the safety car could circulate with the survivors while the track was swept of debris.

"It should have really been red flagged," smiles Mark Webber. "But the Australian was still running and they didn't red flag it and certain things went our way. When Australians have got a job to do they get in and do it in the best way possible. When it's their event on show, the marshals are briefed and do the best job possible and I suppose they were very keen to keep the race going ... they did a good job!"

Paul Stoddart says he now believes in fate. "Just un-un-believable, I don't think there'll ever be another day like it. Here we were thinking 'Well, if Mark can finish top ten, what a party it would be,' and there were so many things that happened that day. First of all, there's the big accident and the red flag doesn't come out. Why doesn't it come out? So much carnage everywhere and we didn't know if our cars had got through, so you're on the radio trying to find out and your next thoughts are 'shit, they're going to red flag it,' and they don't and I didn't find out until later that night as to why they didn't red flag it. On lap three, I'm told on the radio that Mark's car is terminal, it's not going to make another couple of laps, it's got a differential problem and it's going to run out of oil. And we're thinking 'ah, shit' because he was seventh or something, but he keeps going and then we get to the pit stop and they're on the radio saying 'when it comes in, once it stops it ain't going to get going again and get ready to try to push him out but expect it to be terminal'. So he does the stop and gets off on his own power and by now the engineers are saying 'look, technically this car should have stopped 20 laps ago, we don't know what's keeping it going, we give up!' and they're starting to doubt their own telemetry."

Mark and Alex plugged away and in the closing stages it became clear points were on the cards. Toyota was contesting its first Grand Prix and driver Mika Salo hunted Webber. The young Aussie resisted the pressure superbly and, eventually, it was Salo himself who span. Michael Schumacher won the race at a canter and was watching the giant TV screens in the closing stages to check on Minardi's progress. So at what point did it dawn on Mark that points were possible?

"I suppose half-way through the race. I didn't get ahead of myself before that because the car was not very reliable in testing. [After the crash] it was quite a boring Grand Prix but not for the sake of one black car running around in the points. Stoddie said to me on the grid 'Mate, if we can just get the car home it would be a huge achievement.' Salo started to catch me, he'd had problems at the start, he was much much faster and I had problems with the electronics. Basically, the orders were 'under no circumstances should you let Salo past'. Two points is double of what sixth place would have been. I knew the difference between one and two points was going to be massive. The radiator coolant [on which Salo span] was out there in turn three all race, it was from Jenson when he got hit at turn one, so he dropped that coolant and it was there for the last hour and 20 minutes. I had to keep defending down the inside so Salo couldn't pass me. I knew he was very strong on the straight so (laughs) he was going to have to work very hard to pass me!"

"You think about strategy meetings you had," says Stoddart, "Salo's coming up behind him, there's now three laps to go 'oh God, he's not going to be able to hold Salo off, but we'll still get sixth' and then Mika spins. Michael Schumacher told me he had to keep asking his pit if the race was finished because for the last three laps every time he came past he thought the race was over because the crowd were up on their feet. He was looking at the big diamond

Webber and the Minardi PS02 hold off Mika Salo's Toyota. (Courtesy Sutton Motorsport Images)

screens to see if Mark was still going to make it. When he went forward to spray the champagne he said he didn't see many people and then he looked left down to Minardi and the whole pit lane was down there. Mechanics from every team were hanging on the wire when the car crossed the line. It was one of the most unbelievable moments of Formula 1 history. I don't think it'll ever be repeated again, there'll never be a more emotional or important two points."

Yoong was just out of the points in seventh. He could have, should have, got sixth but was being shown too many blue flags by marshals who didn't realise which lap he was on. It was an amazing result for Mark – his first GP and in front of his home fans. After the official podium presentation, organisers allowed Stoddart and Webber up there to soak in the adulation.

"Everyone was bawling their eyes out," says Stoddart. "I said to Mark afterwards 'thank God we have the champagne on the podium because it covers the tears'. In Melbourne now there are still people who believe we won the race!"

"I knew Bernie would have a seizure watching from his armchair at home in London," says Ron Walker. "I also had some trepidation about Max [Mosley] seeing it as well because nobody is allowed to do that sort of thing. Because of the emotion of what happened we got away with it but we fully expected a very rude letter and a fine of £50,000 for breach of protocol ... but it never came."

This was the best it would get. The team owner admits it was "the happiest day of my life, not just my best F1 moment!" He says Schumacher ducked his sponsor duties and found his way to the Minardi celebration at Melbourne's Stoke House; without doubt, the best party in town.

So what of the 'miracle' of turn one? Should the race have been stopped? Did the Australian marshals only do it for the black cars? Paul Stoddart was taken to their party. "One of the turn one marshals said to me 'Paul, you don't realise what we did, do you? You don't know how we cleared the track ...' They'd seen both the Minardis go through and they actually ran out of cranes to move the cars. The last Sauber ... was physically lifted by eight marshals and carried off the track – that's fate, mate."

It's a nice thought but one which doesn't wash with race promoter Ron Walker. "It's arrant nonsense. It had nothing to do with Mark Webber. I mean, Formula 1 is bigger than Mark Webber, Paul Stoddart or Ron Dennis. It is a huge, international circus and whatever the marshals did or didn't do had nothing to do with Mark Webber or Paul Stoddart."

There's also disagreement about whether Ron Walker had

Minardi's podium ... for fifth.
(Courtesy Sutton Motorsport Images)

"In Melbourne now there are still people who believe we won the race!" Paul Stoddart.
(Courtesy Sutton Motorsport Images)

earlier promised to find Australian sponsors if cash-strapped Minardi ran Mark Webber.

"Ron was doing my head in but in a very friendly way," says Stoddart. "He was integral in getting Mark the drive. He said 'Come on Paul, we've got to do this, we've got to make this happen, we'll find some sponsors' and I told him we wouldn't but I wanted to sign Mark anyway ... he did say he was going to get sponsors."

Ron Walker: "'I really don't understand why he says that because nobody in this industry has done more for Paul Stoddart than I have in terms of building him up, giving him confidence, giving him the courage to strike out in a very competitive, bitchy world of Formula 1 where it's dog eat dog in the paddock. For him to say that was a bit disappointing. He's got a big head of his own, he understands the frailties and the risks of Formula 1 the same as everybody else. He knew that I was helping Mark financially and getting sponsors for him. I never, ever undertook to get sponsors for Paul. We have a huge task in gaining sponsors for the Grand Prix itself let alone going out and touting for a team."

Ron Walker says Stoddart failed to find Australian sponsors because of time zones, international television schedules and the lack of airtime received by Minardi. "I wasn't actually surprised he couldn't find a big sponsor. A lot of the major companies in Australia are not into motor racing. It's easy for them to promote the Australian

Webber finished 11th in Brazil. (Courtesy Sutton Motorsport Images)

Open tennis or soccer or rugby or [Aussie Rules] football, but Formula 1 was new to the Australian sponsorship market. We had Qantas lined up for years as the major race sponsor, as we did Fosters, but for them to put money into a team which had limited signage on the side for television purposes just didn't work for them. Fosters beer supported Mark during his apprenticeship years and it was very hard to find people who were prepared to throw big money at us. Telstra sponsored Mark, which was a big leg up for him, but we just couldn't find sponsors for Minardi." The final comment suggests Walker was, indeed, on the lookout for Stoddart, albeit informally.

Surely, after Albert Park, Australian firms would be fighting to get their logos on the black cars? Paul Stoddart says he

Yoong would have an accident in Monaco, but it was one of Webber's best races. (Courtesy Sutton Motorsport Images)

Practice in Spain, before wing failures meant both cars were withdrawn. (Courtesy Simon Vigar)

wasn't holding his breath. "I'd had years of trying to get Australian sponsors on board with Mark. I'd been round the traps and I just knew the serious money wasn't on offer. Some companies went with other teams. Foster's were sponsoring the GP and Mark. An insurance company sponsored Jordan in 1999, that was a serious deal. We never cracked it. Yes, it is the greatest race on the calendar but it's only one race a year and the rest of the season they're out of time zone and, unfortunately, the TV coverage is crap."

So, an Australian driving for an 'Australian' team but very few Australian dollars. Stoddart had been talking with other drivers for 2002 including Christijan Albers (Webber's team-mate in Stoddart's F3000 team) and Justin Wilson, but they would have to wait their turns. Mark Webber secured the seat and says it was a fantastic year with Minardi. "As long as you can remember in car racing there have always been the haves and the have-nots. Minardi are my second favourite team; an incredible, passionate team and virtually family-run. We should have found a balance between the big artillery and also having the teams and characters which bring a lot more passion to the sport. You need the guys at the back there, ready for that rainy day when they can get a phenomenal result which no-one will forget."

Points make Albert Park unforgettable but, for Mark, they were a gift. For the true racer, there were more significant races, even though there were no points.

"At Monte Carlo, the Michelin technicians said the lap times I was doing weren't possible! A few special moments there. In the warm-up, we had a huge amount of fuel and were still 13th or 12th, which was just unheard of. We had to change our strategy because we were getting held up so badly in the race and this is in a Minardi! I was on the radio: 'Guys, we've got to change the strategy, we're getting held up, let's do something different.'" He'd started 19th and finished 11th. Yes, it was a typical Monaco race with many retirements, but the Arrows of Enrique Bernoldi finished behind the Minardi.

It's tough at the top. Alex Yoong in Brazil. (Courtesy Sutton Motorsport Images)

The low points of 2002 included a double 'did not start' in Barcelona. The team packed up because of three wing failures in practice. A manufacturing fault was identified and Paul Stoddart pulled the plug on the weekend.

Most of the season was a low point as far as Alex Yoong is concerned. He knew he was diving in the deep end but had been promised a decent amount of testing. It didn't turn out like that, "I don't know what Paul did with the money and I don't want to speculate but I ended up doing five days testing for the whole one and a half years I was there. That was really rough because it meant I had to do all my learning in the race weekend so it was really, really tough and

Alex and his amazing technicolour dream car. (Courtesy Sutton Motorsport Images)

Magny-Cours two months later was even better: "We were so quick there ... I've never, ever been interested in lucky results. Melbourne was special but we knew how lucky we were. When you have quality behind you, that's what makes you happy and satisfied." Mark finished eighth with his team-mate, a Jaguar and a Toyota behind him. He had earned a drive at Jaguar for 2003 after a 'perfect' first season.

"Even with mechanics and lots of different things, [Minardi] have, in many ways, the grassroots for F1. Obviously, it's not a junior category but Minardi has had Fisichella, Alonso, myself, Trulli, lots of guys have driven for them. No-one was going to take Fernando straight to Renault or McLaren or Ferrari for his first year, or the rest of us. Minardi was the perfect place to start and a great place for us to show the manufacturers what we could do."

the results weren't there. Looking back, it was impossible to get the results."

Drivers don't want sympathy, but Yoong got it from this writer who watched him, confidence shot, cruise into Copse at Silverstone during practice. F1 is for big boys, and Copse is one of the 'big boy' corners on the calendar. Blind exit and nowadays they hardly lift. Having a very good team-mate banging in the times can't have helped. The British GP was one of three where Yoong failed to qualify – 5.7 seconds off pole, he was also 2.5 seconds slower than his team-mate. Over the season the deficit averaged at 1.5.

"It was terrible," says Yoong, "because I could only try things out on race weekends. I never had the chance to sit down with my engineer at a test and work through a programme. I really understood why I was struggling but it's not something I can put into words, it's just a feeling about being able to relax."

Some may argue Webber could have done with a more competitive team-mate, but the Aussie says, at a small team, it really doesn't matter:

"No, because I set my own goals. I had to. It was brilliant to try to out-qualify the Jaguars, I was running seventh or eighth in Monte Carlo ahead of BARs and Saubers. Of course, I couldn't set my goals on comparisons with my team-mate. I had to set my own stall out there. I had to test myself massively and be hyper-competitive against guys, which I am. As Steve Waugh [former Australia cricket captain] always says 'you never play them on their reputation, just go there and do it.'"

Was there sympathy for Alex?

"There were times when it was tough. He did improve mentally over the season because it was much harder at the start and he had a lot of doubts in his own head. I think he got better as the season went on but, in the end, you really felt for the team."

Power steering would have helped. Minardi could initially only afford to run one unit and, understandably, it went to Mark. Stoddart stood by Alex but a third disastrous qualification effort, at Hockenheim, prompted the boss to 'rest' him. "It was the best thing we ever did. It focussed his mind and if he could have been like that all season he'd have had a better year ... he didn't deserve as much criticism as he got. If he'd been in a different team with a bigger budget it might have been a slightly different story. Lack of money had a direct impact on the car. The reason we cancelled a lot of our testing in 2002 was because we didn't have the budget to do it. $13.5m [from Malaysia] is a lot of money to a lot of people, but in Formula 1 it doesn't even scratch the surface so just getting through that year with a total of $22.5m, it wouldn't have paid

Webber at Silverstone. Yoong would fail to qualify for the second time. (Courtesy Sutton Motorsport Images)

McLaren's food bill. [Alex] had more than five days testing in 2001-02 combined but it wasn't ideal."

F3000 champion Justin Wilson would have sat in Yoong's car if he physically could have, but his height at 6ft 3in (1.92m) ruled him out. A very late call was made to fellow Brit and BAR tester Anthony Davidson, who was put in the car for Hungary and Belgium and was immediately within 0.5 second of Webber. His fastest race lap was actually quicker than Mark's, but he span off with only a quarter of the race to go. Webber's insouciance here is wonderful:

"Anthony Davidson did two races and it was a good little marker for me because people were raving about him and actually he wasn't fit enough to do the races, so that was a shame for him. I was disappointed for the team as a whole that the other side of the garage wasn't getting the results they could have."

With refreshing honesty, Davidson agrees with Webber. "I remember doing the first couple of laps of practice in Hungary and I actually thought 'what have I done? This is going to be hard work!" He was 22 and had only just started testing for BAR, a better car than the Minardi. "The car had hardly any power steering and the team had just gone to the Michelin tyre which actually was a lot more physical to drive. I'd been driving the Bridgestone tyre for BAR. It was my first full season of Formula 1 so to jump in mid-season, I'd only done about 15 days total in an F1 car and I'd never done a race distance, I didn't know what to expect at all. I was absolutely hanging on from about 30-40 laps into the race and it was just too much in the end. I just ran out of arm strength."

Davidson now regrets offering to be a very late substitute for Alex Yoong.

At 5ft 3in (1.60m), Davidson is a full foot shorter than Justin Wilson but even he thought the Minardi was a squeeze. "I remember still to this day how tiny even for me the cockpit was. It was a nice little car inside, that's obviously why Justin couldn't get in."

Anthony again ended up in the gravel during the next race at Spa and feared it was the end of his F1 racing career. His mistake was trying to keep up with his old sparring-partner from Formula 3, Takuma Sato. "Mark was out with a gearbox problem so I thought 'you're the last placed guy, you see the car in front of you just starting to edge away, it was Takuma in the Jordan and you just push on'. Coupled with the lack of arm strength round the fast corners, I overcooked it a bit too much. It's very rare for me to make mistakes and I'm surprised no-one really caught on to figure it out. I hadn't gone off in free practice, hadn't gone off at all in my time at BAR in any length of stint and the BAR power steering was easy, like a Playstation. I've never had to have strong arms at all and that's the case today, but that car was so hard to drive."

Apart from his baggy, borrowed overalls, the enduring memory

Even Anthony Davidson found the cockpit cosy.
(Courtesy Sutton Motorsport Images)

Alex Yoong made an impressive comeback at the Italian Grand Prix. (Courtesy Sutton Motorsport Images)

Yoong ahead of Webber into Parabolica. Mark would retire. (Courtesy Sutton Motorsport Images)

of Davidson is how he collected the quickest penalty fine in Grand Prix history as he sped out of the pit lane for the first time. His two outings for Minardi were not the beginning and end of his F1 race career. Five years later, he joined Honda's 'B' team, Super Aguri; a team which, in part, rose from the ashes of Minardi.

A revitalised Alex Yoong returned for the last three races of 2002 and repaired some of the damage to his reputation. He narrowed the qualifying gap with Webber to 0.7 at Indianapolis and 0.3 at Suzuka. "It's weird driving a car. I became very fit in the second half of the season and I was working out very hard twice a day. I don't know what it was but I reached a stage of aerobic fitness where I was able to relax in the car and it's a snowballing effect because you just get better. If you get tired you start tensing and it gets worse and worse. There's a fine line and if you're above that line it's as easy as pie. If you're below

Alex Yoong and his GoKL sponsorship at their last race in Japan. (Courtesy Sutton Motorsport Images)

it's painful, really painful ... there were a few people in the team who really worked hard with me and that's why I was able to walk away from F1 with my head held high. Those people understood we'd reached a good finishing point, although the press and the wider population would never know about it." In 2005, Alex fronted Malaysia's successful entry into the new A1GP series and, through that, raced impressively at Le Mans.

Minardi did not receive all the Malaysian money, but 2002 was proving far tougher for larger teams. Prost went bust before the season began, and Arrows became a travelling circus. Through grim financial necessity, Paul Stoddart became an expert on the Concorde agreement, the secret document which governs Formula 1. His battle for the revenue due to the defunct Prost outfit became known as 'Prostgate' and involved a fight with Arrows boss Tom Walkinshaw, who set up a phantom team called Phoenix. Phoenix bought the old Prost cars and the commercial rights of the team; would that be enough for Walkinshaw to get his hands on the cash? No, and Minardi, eventually, received about half of the Prost money.

"I had a monumental fight with Tom over the TV money. Phoenix rose from the ashes of Prost, what an appropriate name that was. I laughingly refer to Tom as 'Arthur Daley' [a fictional wheeler-dealer character on British TV] but that was the lowest of the low, turning up in Melbourne with a pair of nose cones and expecting Charlie [Whiting of the FIA] to scrutinise them and get his way through the Concorde agreement was just never going to happen. I had to fight very hard that year because with the

Seen any Russian money recently? The Gazprom men at Monza. (Courtesy Sutton Motorsport Images)

alaysian money down, with no TV money coming, it's arguable hether we would have actually got through if it wasn't for Mosley's lp. Max interpreted Concorde absolutely correctly and that money longed to Minardi."

July was the month of reckoning for Arrows. On the seventh, -one knew if they'd even turn up for their home race at verstone. At Magny-Cours on the 21st, embattled team principal m Walkinshaw ordered his cars to go out yet not qualify. The zarre spectacle meant he was still honouring the letter of his ntracts, if not the spirit. Hockenheim one week later was the last and Prix for Arrows, the team which holds the record no-one ants: 382 races without a win. Minardi came close.

Stoddart, of course, had tried to buy Arrows in 2000. "Due diligence didn't even last two days, I was told 'this is going down don't touch it with a bargepole'. I was aware of their problems. Later on, with bloody Prostgate, it didn't surprise me at all. It's fu because at times I could have killed Tom but, in actual fact, we s speak with each other, there's no grudges borne, I just feel sorry the staff ... bad management ends up landing innocent people in mess. His mistake was to underestimate the amount of money y need in modern F1. He never had the budget yet he kept spendi the money, it was debt upon debt upon debt. It was never going work ... he probably crossed the line [legally] on one occasion ar he got himself into an absolutely hopeless position where a lot o very good people, innocent people are still very bitter to this day because they got very, very badly bruised."

Far more illustrious teams than Arrows fell by the wayside during Minardi's 21 seasons. Gian Carlo Minardi says the secret was to stick to a staff of about 100: "Other teams, growing to 250-300 employees, made a mistake because in tough moments they didn't have enough money and had to give up."

The chaos strengthened Paul Stoddart's hand in negotiations. F1 ringmaster Bernie Ecclestone promised the circuits and the promoters 20 cars on the grid and was now down to that bare minimum. Could he persuade the big teams to run three cars if Minardi also went to the wall? Would the third cars score points for the constructor? What if they impeded rival cars? It was a can of worms and both Bernie and Paul knew it. He would now use this leverage to get any cash he could from the big boys. Sometimes it worked, sometimes it didn't.

'Go KL' didn't go on the cars in 2003. Rumours of rich benefactors teased Minardi every now and then – at the end of 2002 it was the Russian power giant Gazprom. Although the logo appeared on the cars at the start of 2003, the hard cash didn't.

A nice post-script to the season is linked to that glorious day at the very start. At the party in Melbourne, Paul Stoddart had promised Michael Schumacher a day in a Minardi two-seater, albeit painted red. The champion wanted his wife Corinna and other family and friends to experience the power of a Formula 1 car. "Bridgestone gave us some tyres for the day at Fiorano and Michael proved to me why he's a seven time world champion," says Stoddart. "Fernando had lapped Fiorano at 1:02:11 in the 2001 race car and Michael lapped it at 1:04:2 in the two-seater with passengers."

2003

Going nuts in Brazil

"I couldn't talk, Jos couldn't talk. OK, it's easy to be wise after the event because had the race gone 100 per cent, the strategy wouldn't have worked; had it not been run under safety car, we'd have run out of fuel; but, as it did pan out, it was 50 per cent under the safety car, it did go 75 per cent distance, we did have enough fuel to do that race. Had Jos stayed on the black stuff, he would have won. No questions, 100 per cent he'd have won."

For Paul Stoddart, April 6th 2003 is the day his Minardi team should have won a race and three Minardi 'old boys' would have played leading roles, as would the weather, in an echo of Adelaide '89 and Nürburgring '99. The Brazilian Grand Prix at Interlagos was a bizarre affair run in torrential conditions, and on the climb up the hill to the pit-straight Mark Webber crashed his Jaguar. Fernando Alonso then had a huge shunt in his Renault after hitting one of the Jaguar's stray tyres, stopping the race. This meant, on countback, the victory was eventually awarded to Giancarlo Fisichella.

Like Minardi, Jordan's strategy for Fisichella was to fill the tank to the brim, cut down on pit stops and pray for several safety car periods to conserve fuel. He was dead last after his pit stop but went on to score his first and Jordan's last victory.

So what of Jos Verstappen? He was ahead of the Jordan and on the same 'fingers crossed' strategy for much of the race. Indeed, Fisichella couldn't catch him, but Verstappen span out in the cross-

"Jos the Boss" with his engineer Greg Wheeler. (Courtesy Sutton Motorsport Images)

"No questions, 100% he'd have won." Verstappen in the deluge at Interlagos. (Courtesy Sutton Motorsport Images)

track torrent at Curva do Sol and claimed several others, including team-mate Justin Wilson and Michael Schumacher. The anti-stall device failed to kick in and it was race over. Stoddart asserts it's the only time in Minardi's history the team started a race with a realistic hope of winning. "Minardi was potentially in a genuine, race-winning position. Only those of us within the team will ever know the truth. We had the strategy but not the luck.

"Minardi should have won. I know we could have won it, we had the strategy. I didn't often interfere with the race engineers but that morning I went in and it was an absolute torrential downpour and I said 'I reckon we can get points here, let's fuel that T-car to the gunnels, I don't reckon this race is going to last the distance, we might even spend the whole race behind the safety car. If we've got the fuel and we can just stay out there longer they're going to have to peel in for fuel, this is going to be a one stop strategy and we might even get through on a no stop strategy.' And they all said 'you're fucking crazy' and I said 'I'm not, you know I don't normally interfere with you but I am telling you this is what we're doing, I'm not asking you, I'm telling you, so you can toss a coin between the

In eight seasons, Verstappen fans argue he never had a car to show what he could do. (Courtesy Sutton Motorsport Images)

drivers to see who gets the T-car.' Jos said 'don't be stupid,' but I said trust me. The most stupid thing of all took us both out on turn three and in both cases the anti-stall didn't pick it up because it was a high speed stall. No damage and two stalled cars; un-fucking-believable. I've never lost my temper so much in a race. The pitwall is so high in Brazil, we're like six foot above the track, I grabbed my radio and I threw the fucking thing across the pit lane and it slammed into the barriers in the back of the garage. You couldn't speak to anybody at Minardi for two hours, you've never seen such a silent pack-up. People couldn't talk. We knew we had the fuel to finish. We would have won, no question. We didn't have to stop, we got the strategy right, we knew that half the race would be under the safety car and it'd stop at 75 per cent distance. I didn't know that Fernando would slam into the wall and cause the red flag but I figured something would. We didn't need to stop. One by one they'd have peeled off and we'd have won the race. I said to Fisi that night on the plane 'if Jos had been in front of you and you were in second, would you have tried to overtake him? And he said 'try to overtake a Minardi that was about to win a race? Are you stupid?!'" Stoddart can laugh now.

Justin Wilson had earlier gone off at the same water-logged spot "Unfortunately, this anti-stall put us both out of the race. We both managed to keep it out of the wall, many people didn't, but the anti-stall refused to let us drive on. I was gutted; I was so disappointed that I'd fallen off. It wasn't until I got back to the pits that I found out five other people had done the same thing. I felt a little bit better about myself at that point."

Kudos and headlines apart, the win would have had huge financial implications. As it was, post-September 11th, the sponsorship situation was now critical. The season had started with much fanfare and hope and Gian Carlo was still working hard on a multi-year deal with the Russians. Paul Stoddart thought the Gazprom money along with expensive Cosworth engines would help Minardi turn the corner. "Great things were supposed to happen, but by March [Gazprom] had defaulted ... so the $50m budget was reduced to $28m, so what had to go? The R&D."

Points on the board in 2002 meant there was no problem with the payment from Formula One Management (FOM); Minardi received $15m. Another boost was a change to qualifying. Now it would be one car at a time meaning more TV airtime for the small teams and their sponsors.

Jos Verstappen attracted $1.5m from Dutch firms, principally computer company Trust, and more would follow. Stoddart also signed Minardi's first full-time British driver, Justin Wilson. An unassuming Yorkshireman, Justin actually sold shares in himself to raise the required $2m.

"You pay your money and you take your chance," says Wilson. "You believe in yourself, you hope you can do what Mark and Fernando did. It's the risk you take. Maybe you get a bit of luck, you get the break and the timing is right ... We were over-optimistic but you have to be positive in these situations. Also, we had the Cosworth which was about 100 horsepower up on what they'd had. We thought we'd be stronger than we were and with a little bit of luck could come out with a surprising result [like Albert Park]." Later in the season Wilson would drive the Jaguar-Cosworth, putting him in the perfect position to quash rumours Minardi was receiving significantly inferior engines. "[Maybe it was 25hp down] you can't really feel it that much; it works out 100hp for about a second a lap; so 25hp was maybe 3/10 over the course of a lap which, unfortunately, was not what we were missing! The biggest thing was everyone had moved forward so much with [aerodynamics] in the off season. The Jaguar was much more stable, a much quicker car. We had that optimism before the season started and unfortunately we didn't move on at all and everyone else had, so it just meant we were struggling."

Justin had struggled to get into a Formula 1 car, literally. Also known as 'The Flying Giraffe', his 6ft 3in frame (1.92m) had prevented him landing the Minardi drive for 2002. It went to Mark Webber, the man Justin had just beaten to the F3000 crown. Undeterred, Paul Stoddart tried to squeeze him in as replacement for Alex Yoong in the middle of 2002, but that didn't work either. Stoddart told Wilson not to give up hope, and that they would adjust the chassis for 2003 if Wilson could come up with the cash.

Justin says the ageing car only needed tweaks like moving the pedals. "If it was going to affect performance in any way there was no point in me doing it ... they did a couple of things but they were pretty small. I don't think it compromised the performance of the car. It was tight but it was manageable – they gave me some

Justin Wilson talking down to his engineer, Alex Varnava. (Courtesy Sutton Motorsport Images)

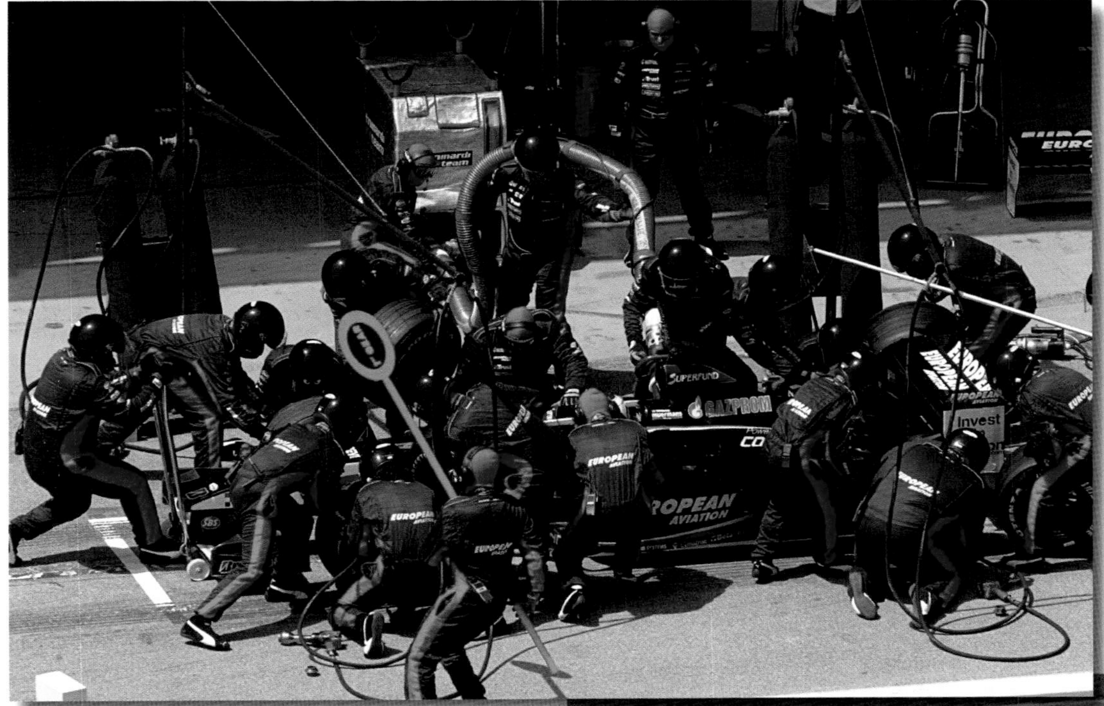

A great little team.
(Courtesy Sutton Motorsport Images)

tight, we didn't get any testing. I guess my expectations were just that and anything else was a bonus. It was in at the deep end and you're just trying to stay alive for those first few races. You don't know the tracks, you don't know the car and everything's happening a bit fast. As soon as you get to something familiar, like Barcelona, you then feel at home in the car, rather than everything feeling alien. You relax a little bit so you can do more than just drive the car, you can process more data."

Wilson outshone his more experienced team-mate with some blinding starts.

"It's a number of things that come together – we're starting from the back so have nothing to lose and because we're

Nick Heidfeld can't believe he's another of Justin Wilson's opening lap victims.
(Courtesy Sutton Motorsport Images)

more clearance on my knees. [The media's obsession with my height] got really boring; you just want to focus on driving but there's so much going on in the background, people focussed on the height and they naturally thought that's what held me back. There wasn't much I could do about it."

Before the season even started there was an embarrassing stand-off, during which both tyre companies refused to supply little Minardi. Bridgestone relented but not before a risible test using some old F3000 Avon slicks. Justin Wilson denies it started to ring alarm bells. He laughs "I just thought 'this is messy,' but I had confidence in Paul that he would sort it out and he did."

Like Alex Yoong the year before, Justin's only time in the car was during a race weekend. "We knew things were a little behind, everyone gets to the first corner and has their little moment and you can take the corner at full racing speed so you can take advantage of people. Also, I've learned to be quite 'heads-up' and working out where the gap's going to be and trying to get the timing just right. That's part of who I am and what I do and what I enjoy. I remember once passing Ralf and thinking 'this shouldn't really happen!' It didn't last very long but I had to take every opportunity I had. Also, at Barcelona, I passed Heidfeld."

Every fan wants to know what it's like for the driver caught up in the melee of a first lap in Formula 1. Are they smiling behind those visors as they cut through the pack? Are they even laughing? "At the time you're pretty cool," says Justin. "You're just working out what's next. 'OK, I've passed him, how am I going to get the next guy?' You're thinking ahead and it's only afterwards you chuckle to yourself 'that was fun'."

Jos Verstappen had, by now, developed 'a bit of a reputation', but Wilson feels 'Jos the Boss' gets a bad rap. "At first he was very wary of me, he didn't like younger team-mates. I think it was his previous experience at Arrows or something. He was very wary that I was trying to take advantage or put one over on him or do something. It was probably five or six races into the season when he warmed to me a little and realised that I wasn't trying to be sneaky or do anything our of order and then we got on really well. I really like Jos and he was a good team-mate."

The eyes have it. Jos in Canada. (Courtesy Sutton Motorsport Images)

The PS03 bore a striking resemblance to the PS02 and the PS04B. They were one and the same. (Courtesy Sutton Motorsport Images)

Again, Magny-Cours was a highlight where, thanks to a drying track, Minardi claimed the front row in Friday qualifying. Verstappen took provisional P1, but Wilson's car was underweight so his time was scrubbed. P1 was as fun as it was insignificant.

The defining moment of Paul Stoddart's career as an F1 team principal came at Montreal where the big teams denied him access to the 'fighting fund', designed to prevent another Prost/Arrows-style meltdown. Stoddart thought Eddie Jordan was on side until a spectacular news conference when it became obvious the Irishman had been got at with the promise of engines from Mercedes. In previous seasons, Ron Dennis and Frank Williams had been helping Minardi with tyre bills. Perhaps this explains their contempt for Stoddart at the heated news conference and their observation that Formula 1 is no soup kitchen.

"We fell out in 2003 because of the fighting fund and the broken promises," says Stoddart. "It was promised on January 15th, it was reaffirmed specifically by Ron in April 29th and it was just not happening. By the time of Montreal I was so desperate because Minardi really was going to go under, we had nothing left and we needed the money that had been pledged to us. We'd done things and weren't getting a fair go. If I hadn't spoken out, Minardi would have finished that weekend. It was the first time I really thought the doors were going to shut, we were in so much shit. I had a meeting with Eddie on the Wednesday and he said 'Yes, you've got to fight for us, we're both in the shit here, Jordan's going to go down as well' and he said 'I'm right behind you, mate', I remember the words so well!" laughs Stoddart.

Cruise control; both cars retire in Monaco with 'fuel feed' problems.
(Courtesy Sutton Motorsport Images)

P1 in Q1 on a drying track in France. (Courtesy Sutton Motorsport Images)

"Whether it be business or sport or anything else, my responsibility was never to Minardi," says Eddie. "My responsibility was to my staff and my people and hence I stand by what I did. At that stage I had no engine and I needed to be guaranteed one. I was basically told 'Jordan, shut up and we can help you to get this contract in place.' Without an engine you can't go motor racing. I got the engine and I had to bite my lip."

Except he didn't get the engine. The plan for a price-capped Mercedes engine, to be re-branded 'Smart' after Merc's small car subsidiary, fell through at the last minute. As the manufacturers continued their

Stoddart lets rip in Canada. (Courtesy Sutton Motorsport Images)

"Well, things happened so quickly," says Jordan. "Paul was busy with the press, they were in love with him, he was the total underdog and there was a bit of antipathy for the major teams [and I agreed] but a deal was struck for me. I have the responsibility of looking after my team, I had to change a view that I had, that he thought I had. I wasn't able to tell him my view had changed and, of course, he went on to call me Judas and that's his prerogative, no problem."

"It was pretty clear on the Friday morning that Eddie was being got at and I do now know exactly what happened. When Eddie turned up with all the other principals and Bernie seven minutes late for the press conference I could see in Eddie's face that something had happened. This is where he got the nickname Judas Jordan because, instead of backing me up, he did everything but and launched into his speech about how Jordan is its own team, has won races and it doesn't want charity from anyone."

Formation Minardis at the Nürburgring. (Courtesy Sutton Motorsport Images)

campaign for more cash and more say, they tried to build a strong alliance against FOM (Ecclestone) and the FIA (Mosley). One consequence was no 'gifts' for the small guys and Ford leant on Mercedes to drop the Jordan deal. It meant Eddie had to go with Ford Cosworth in 2004 and it's now clear this was the beginning of the end, not only for Jordan, but Sauber and Minardi too. The last 'independent' teams all bowed out in 2005. What irony that the following year Honda created a 'B' team in Super Aguri amid similar plans by McLaren-Mercedes/Prodrive. Just get shot of the genuine privateers ...

After the 2003 Montreal news conference, Stoddart and Bernie announced Ecclestone had become a shareholder in Minardi. The bottom line for Bernie was his grid was down to the bare minimum of 20 cars – he couldn't afford to watch another team go to the wall. Promoters, for once, would have been able to turn the tables on Bernie and exercise penalty clauses in the contracts. "The truth is it never happened," confirms Ecclestone. "I said I would lend [Minardi] money and I would take the shares over to secure the money and sell the shares back to them when they repaid the debt at the end of the year. If not I would just wind the company up. No money changed hands, nothing at all." Classic Bernie; money's nowhere near as powerful as influence.

Paul Stoddart agrees, but he says being linked with Bernie at the time helped him no end with suppliers and creditors who suddenly became more amenable. "On Friday the 13th of June 2003 he offered to help. Bernie would've gone ahead with that deal to buy half of Minardi. As it turned out, he said to me a month or two later 'Paul, you don't need me to do this now, do you?' and I said 'No, I don't.' When I needed someone to help me and turned around, Bernie was there. And it wasn't the first time he'd

300th GP celebration at the Hungaroring. Minardi drivers include (left to right) Campos, Alonso, Webber, Verstappen, Wilson, Trulli, Kiesa and Bruni. (Courtesy Sutton Motorsport Images)

helped me, or Eddie or other people for that matter."

Paul Stoddart seemed to revel in the attention but it appalled Gian Carlo Minardi – after all, his name was still above the door.

"We didn't have an easy relationship. He had his own strategy. In any case, my presence was difficult for him. We had several discussions. I explained to him my point of view. But, unfortunately, I didn't have many options. He was the boss. I could disassociate myself from him, as I did on many occasions, even in public."

And in public, Bernie was full of disdain for what Stoddart was doing to 'the show', even telling him to pack up and go home. This is Bernie's response when asked if he pitied Minardi's plight: "The bottom line is simple; you've got to be there with the finance to support the team properly. Unless you can do that, you're never going to be successful and you're never going to get the right sponsorship." That is the story of Minardi in a nutshell.

Remember Ecclestone's cryptic verdict on Stoddart, "We all know what Paul was, we all know exactly what the difference between him and Gian Carlo was. We had an awful lot of trouble with Stoddart and we had none with Gian Carlo."

"Absolutely," says the Australian. "Gian Carlo used to just say 'yes sir, no sir, three bags full', mainly because of the language and secondly because he felt Minardi was not able to do anything other than just take the crumbs that were thrown to it and many, many times Minardi got screwed over. There are documents that I've seen that him and Rumi signed that, while my arsehole pointed

Paul Stoddart and Murray Walker. (Courtesy Sutton Motorsport Images)

to the ground, would never have got a signature from me, and it clearly disadvantaged them."

There was never a dull moment with Paul Stoddart around, making friends and enemies with ease. One of his firmest friendships was with the doyen of Grand Prix commentators, Murray Walker.

"Paul used to fly me to the races from Bournemouth airport, which is near my home. We would go in Citroën Picassos to the race and then we would drive back to the aerodrome and fly home. Paul is not a bloke who puts up with being held up in any way in life, and we were coming back from Monza one year and were trying to filter into the traffic jam in order to get to the airport, and there was a policewoman standing at the bonnet. Paul was edging forward all the time and she was taking steps back all the time. She was saying 'NO … NO … NOO …. NOOOO!' and all of a sudden she produced a revolver. She pointed it at Paul and said 'NO!' and I said 'Paul, I don't think she wants you to go any further,'" laughs Murray. "That's the sort of bloke he was. He is a major, major loss to the sport."

On track, a season which had started with so much promise had become the usual anticlimax. Justin Wilson headed to Jaguar mid-season in an F1 cul-de-sac (he later built a successful career in American Champ Cars). What does he say to those drivers, like Anthony Davidson, who turned their noses up at Minardi and other 'small teams' (only to end up in Super Aguri in 2007)?

"If the timing's not working for you, you've got to make something happen. You've got to risk failing rather than not trying at all. For me it's been a tough road but it's got me to where I am."

Young Dane Nicholas Kiesa had the budget ready and waiting and raced from Hockenheim onward, but the more impressive arrival in the Minardi garage that summer was Italian tester Gianmaria 'Gimmi' Bruni. Jos Verstappen was by now thoroughly demotivated and certainly didn't appreciate the attention being lavished on the youngster. "He was a little bit upset," says Bruni. "With ten minutes to go of practice at Indy I was four tenths of a second quicker than him and 1.2 quicker than Kiesa. So I finished my programme but my engineer said 'we have another set of soft tyres, do you want to do another run?' So I said yes. We had them on but Jos came on the radio and said 'can I use those tyres? I want to go quicker.' So he got them but he didn't go quicker than me! It was good, I learnt a lot from him."

The second half of 2003 all got a little messy money-wise, and Jos stomped off into involuntary F1 retirement. Happily, in Durban in 2006, his never-say-die attitude ensured his first win in years in the fledgling A1 GP series.

Gimmi Bruni would be signed up for 2004, and it didn't take long for him to reach Verstappen levels of frustration.

2004

Back Indy points

"Bernie said to me 'Max is fucking you every which way and you don't even know it.'"

2004 was the beginning of the end for Paul Stoddart and Minardi. He was already examining offers to buy the team and the politics were about to get even worse, but the biggest blow was the death of his friend and right hand man, John Walton. That's not to say there wasn't cause for optimism; everyone is, at least publicly, optimistic at the start of a season. Yes, it was the same old basic car from 2002 and 2003, but there was more money around. Gianmaria Bruni, Minardi's first Italian driver since Luca Badoer, brought almost $4m and Hungary's Zsolt Baumgartner even more. There was the TV money too, simply for coming tenth in a championship of ten.

Sponsorship was still Dutch, with a twist. Bathroom manufacturer Wilux effectively sub-let some space on the cars to third parties. It never worked and went pear-shaped during the weekend of the British Grand Prix. Minardi's sporting director John Walton had died of cancer. He was hugely popular in the paddock, having worked for five teams including Jordan, where he had met his partner Louise Goodman, later a reporter for British broadcaster ITV. Stoddart decided to replace all decals on the cars with a tribute to 'John Boy'. It was a nice touch but Wilux didn't agree.

Paul Stoddart and his right hand man John Walton at the 2002 British Grand Prix, two years before John-boy's death. (Courtesy Sutton Motorsport Images)

"Apart from being a good mate, [John] was fundamental to the team, he was my eyes and ears in Faenza and it just floored all of us. No words can say it. [Then there was] the reaction of one arsehole sponsor, Ruud Wildschut from Wilux. I felt taking the logos off was the appropriate thing to do and that guy was seriously in default of his money and he used it as an excuse to kill the sponsorship, which was one of the lowest things I've ever seen in my life."

Eddie Jordan and John-boy went way back, to younger, wilder days in Dublin and Formula Three. "I'm not sure if I have the capabilities in terms of my language to describe how unbelievable this man was. He dedicated his life to whatever was his chosen thing, when he was with Jordan he was absolutely faultless ... he was a very strong character, in every way, he liked a drink, he liked girls, but they were all parked to one side when he was motor racing so he was a real man's man. He left to go to Renault and Benetton and then came and set the whole Jordan F1 thing up. I'm indebted to this man. He was a major star and a huge loss."

A minute's silence. (Courtesy Sutton Motorsport Images)

"John ran the race team," says Gimmi Bruni. "He was a very important person to me, he was the only guy who really knew about motor racing. When I was frustrated he would talk to me. I remember we were walking past the FIA guys and one said to John 'when are you going to give this guy a quick car because he needs it,' and John

Taking the PS: the PS04B in Australia was emphatically not a new car. (Courtesy Sutton Motorsport Images)

said 'I know, but unfortunately we don't have enough money to give it to him.' He was a really clever guy, very straight and very focussed on his job and it was a really big shock for Minardi and especially for me when he died. During the race, we were speaking on the radio and he was very important to me. You only have a few people in this world who are good to you and treat you as you are, and he was the only one at Minardi. He was the only one who understood me really well."

"Everybody had the ultimate respect for John," says Minardi mechanic Matt Goodwin, "the Italians and the English, he was the go-between. When he died it was a big, big loss for the team. Everybody was really upset. The impact was massive, it was a big black cloud over the whole event, we couldn't believe it and it had a massive impact on the running of the team."

The beginning of the end for the 'Max and Paul Show'. (Courtesy Sutton Motorsport Images)

Minardi had lost John Boy, and to the bemusement of everyone, including himself, Paul's strong alliance with FIA president Max Mosley also began to deteriorate. "It went wrong on May 8th when, for whatever reason best known to Max, he changed his strategy. Formula 1 needed the independent teams and they were fundamental to the future, and that was a statement he'd made time and time again. The frustration he had with the bigger teams was he could never get the cost cuts through because, within Concorde, there are protections every which way but lose and if you really want to not do something, Concorde is the greatest

The last of the independents. Jordan, Stoddart and Sauber at Imola.
(Courtesy Sutton Motorsport Images)

document I've ever seen in my life to make sure that nothing happens. I became pretty much the paddock expert on Concorde, and not necessarily through choice but through necessity.

"Max was trying desperately to save the teams from themselves. [He knew the manufacturers would eventually abandon F1]. He saw the small teams were fundamental to the future and we were being priced out of Formula 1. Max fought bloody hard – I give credit where credit is due – to bring in change that would lessen the cost of engines, that would guarantee the survival of the independents and give them a chance to compete. Nobody wanted to see half a dozen also-rans and I think the demise of Prost and Arrows really sharpened Max's mind on the fact we were now down to ten teams and all the contracts said no fewer than ten. If another one went, it was going to affect the series in a very bad way."

Stoddart's analysis is that Mosley's exasperation with the big teams and Concorde degenerated into a general disenchantment. Sadly, repeated interview requests to the FIA failed to bear fruit, but it's fair to say Max Mosley believes Paul Stoddart was seduced by the bigger teams and 'went native'.

"Max gave up on bringing through change in an appropriate way and had gone off to look at other ways of doing it. The name 'Mad Max' came from the May meeting. We went in thinking it was just another meeting and came out not knowing what the hell we'd just heard. There were things that were so outrageous and so outside of Concorde we all just thought 'this is not the same Max, what's happened?'"

Mosley was proposing V8 engines to reduce speeds, which he achieved for the 2006 season. Chassis sharing and a single tyre supplier – which, in effect, is what happened the following year – and a mandatory FIA Electronic Control Unit for all engines, anathema to the big manufacturers but projected for introduction in 2008. All of this under the banner of cutting costs and helping the small teams. While Stoddart liked some of it, he was worried about the cost of change and even more worried about Max's attitude.

"This was the bloody marker going down saying 'right, I've had a gutful of you lot, you won't change, you won't do anything to save yourselves so, sod the lot of you, I'm gonna change it.'"

Minardi and the other independents, Sauber and Jordan, met with Mosley at the Monaco Grand Prix. Stoddart says he promised to help the small teams. An exasperated Mosley later tendered his resignation but, at Magny-Cours, Stoddart met with him asking him not to leave the sport.

"Tony Purnell [of Jaguar and Cosworth] told me not to worry about engines; 'you'll be fine, you can race the V10. Max has said whatever they come up with, we'll turn your wick up.' We were told to keep our mouths shut. Then, in China, Ford announces it's pulling out of Formula 1, the whole thing turns upside down. Eddie lost his temper with Ford big time and, of course, this is very unnerving stuff." Eddie Jordan was now ready to go. Throughout the 1990s he'd warned about the influence of the major manufacturers and how they didn't really care about Formula 1. Jordan rightly felt the way he was treated by Honda, Mercedes and Ford proved his point.

The irony is not lost on Stoddart that the very measures designed to protect the small teams and, importantly, encourage new outfits led to him selling up in 2005. He believed as soon as there were more than ten teams in the World Championship, Minardi would be at the bottom of the pile, with no cheque from Bernie's TV fund. The reason he was so gloomy is he knew the 'new teams' would be junior partners to much larger outfits. Formula 1 is a constructors' championship; it is the world's premier racing category because designing and building your own car is what sets it out from the rest. However, there are ways and means, and it was clear that Mosley wanted more teams. He got them in 2006, and both caused ructions. Red Bull purchased Minardi, renamed it Scuderia Toro Rosso and was indeed allowed to continue using V10s. In 2007, both Toro Rosso and Honda's B team Super Aguri ran cars bearing striking similarities to those of the parent companies. It caused outrage among traditionalists like Sir Frank Williams. The new teams simply claimed they weren't buying cars 'off the shelf', but purchasing the intellectual property rights from the parent corporations. Under Concorde, the traditionalists were almost certainly correct, but they didn't get very far. A McLaren-Mercedes 'B' team run by Prodive was expected to join the 2008 FIA Formula 1 World Championship, filling the 12th and final slot. However, Prodrive boss David Richards put plans on hold at the last minute amid continuing uncertainty about Concorde and the B-teams. The whole sorry mess is summed up by the fate of the last 'independant', a team which appeared to be permanently on the market. In the space of four years Jordan became 'Midland', then 'Spyker' and then 'Force India' for 2008. After much wrangling, a deal was agreed to share the pot of cash between the teams which finished 9th, 10th and 11th.

2004 seemed cursed; technical failures mounted, pit fires ignited and at Spa both Minardis were innocent victims of separate crashes. It didn't help that the car was a dog. An old dog. "The few times I beat Jordan in qualifying, it was like winning a race", smiles Gimmi Bruni. "[Getting to F1] was like a dream come true. From when I was a kid, I wanted to be in Formula 1. When I reached

Gimmi Bruni and Zsolt Baumgartner introduced to the Indy crowd by Derek Daly. (Robert Murphy)

Gimmi at Indy. (Courtesy Robert Murphy)

that goal I was the happiest guy in the world. On the other hand, it was difficult for me because I couldn't show what I could do. It's frustrating to think about it even now. I could still be there and be quicker than some drivers but obviously I didn't have the chance to show with the right car."

Bruni is not the first nor the last driver to feel bruised by the top category.

So why did he fail to make Minardi work for him in the way it had for Fisichella, Trulli and Alonso? "Very easy: when they arrived at Minardi they already had a contract with Briatore. I didn't have anybody behind me. It's only luck, they met the right person at the right time. Briatore is a very powerful man in Formula 1.

"When Paul phoned me and said 'you have a chance to be in Formula 1', that was the best time for me. After the first three races though it was very difficult to keep the motivation because I realised I didn't have any more chance to improve. You can imagine how frustrating it was. It was a three year old car and a three year old engine. It was the same car Mark Webber had been driving in 2002." A rumoured new car never materialised.

"All I could do was beat my team-mate in qualifying, that's it, and hope for an easy race, but it was difficult. Nobody was looking after me. Even when you are 9⁄10ths or one second quicker than your team-mate it's good for you but not good for others [in the paddock]. If you look at Lewis Hamilton [at the start of the 2007 season] I

Zsolt Baumgartner scored Minardi's last 'proper' point at Indianapolis. (Robert Murphy)

Italian sunshine. Gianmaria Bruni flanked by his race engineer Riccardo Adami (left) and Minardi's stalwart technical director Gabriele Tredozi. (Courtesy Sutton Motorsport Images)

agree he's a very talented driver but he's with McLaren. If he was with Spyker, I'm sure he couldn't show anything."

And when the 'easy race' materialised at Indianapolis, Bruni was already out of the equation. "I was happy for the team but it was a joke race. I'd been criticised by Paul Stoddart for crashing in the first corners. I qualified 18th, I crashed [with Pantano] at turn one and was stuck in the gravel, but I was happy for the team and Zsolt, he's a good guy."

Yes, the silver lining to 2004 was Baumgartner's point at the US Grand Prix. As others fell by the wayside, he plugged away to come home eighth. Under the new FIA system it was a points-paying position. After his last pit stop Zsolt was 11th, but Webber, Heidfeld and finally Fisichella all dropped out, prompting joyous celebrations at the friendly end of the pit lane. Even Bernie Ecclestone sauntered down. The F1 ringmaster couldn't resist a dig at Stoddart for pouring champagne into plastic cups, 'typical Minardi!'

Race winner Michael Schumacher was asked if he remembered how he felt on his first ever podium and answered: "Like Minardi today. They scored a point. For them, it's sort of like a victory." It was and, excepting the aberration of Indy 2005, it was the last time Minardi scored points in a race proper.

Paul Stoddart: "Before Indy, we'd had a few problems with

"It couldn't have happened to a nicer guy." (Courtesy Sutton Motorsport Images)

Gimmi. Zsolt was incredibly popular with the team because he's just one of life's genuine nice guys. I think Gimmi felt he was the quicker driver, felt he should have had more attention than he got and the truth is Zsolt was incredibly liked by the team, he's a sensible driver. He treated the equipment with respect and it really paid off for him in the States, couldn't have happened to a nicer guy."

It provokes a rueful laugh from Bruni, "Maybe what he says is true. I don't have good memories about it ... it makes me a little bit upset. Nobody cared about me, nobody was looking after me. I couldn't show what I could do."

His reputation was undoubtedly good, which Gimmi confirmed as a Friday tester for Minardi in 2003. He says it was very difficult to hustle the car, to push it to the maximum. A setup for a fast qualifying time would induce oversteer in the race. "It was very unbalanced, very hard to go on the limit. If you were on Zsolt's base setting the car was good. If you were going faster, it was much more difficult. Problems worsened for the tyres and the gearbox."

By the time Gimmi realised he was overly concerned with blitzing Zsolt in qualifying, it was probably too late. He likens the lack of technical progress during the season to an F3000 outfit, not Formula 1.

He wasn't too impressed with Zsolt at Spa but, by then, it was pretty much over anyway. "I qualified 17th in the wet, I beat one Toyota, two Jordans and my team-mate and some other cars which had to change their engines. I made a good start, I was 14th going through Eau Rouge, Sato span in front of me, I backed off, everybody slowed down except for my team-mate and he pushed me into the gravel. Even then, Paul didn't say anything to Zsolt." Well, he had his own problems when he was taken out by Jenson Button's disintegrating car in a scary accident at Les Combes.

A pit fire in Monza ("no-one could tell me what caused it") was followed by high-speed terror rides in Shanghai. His left front tyre came off not once, but twice. "I had a puncture, we changed front left and two laps later I lost it. Tried to go back, change it, go out again, two laps later I lost it again. It was a joke and Paul was telling me 'try to come back,' but I couldn't. I made two corners without the tyre and the whole front disc was destroyed and I was touching on the tarmac and I parked the car. For him it was easy, maybe he likes to do these things but these were the same tyres at 320kmh! Nobody would tell me what the problems were, giving the problem to different people; I called it the 'snake tour' [around the garage]."

Gimmi and Paul turned the air blue when their argument on the team radio was broadcast to the world. The season finale would be the Brazilian Grand Prix.

"Gimmi's the first and only driver that ever refused to qualify a car in my time. It's quite funny actually, when Gimmi was due to go out I was in a meeting with Todt and Bernie, so I had no idea what was happening on the track. We had our normal strategy [it was Gimmi's turn for the heavier load] and he refused to take the car out. I came out and the journalists told me 'Gimmi's had an electrical problem' but my radio was switched off, I was in Todt's office. I got up there and said 'what's wrong with the car' and the engineer said 'nothing', 'what do you mean 'nothing'?' He said 'he don't want to fucking drive. He's pissed off.' And that's when I had the row with Gimmi, I told him if that's the way he felt he could just fuck off home."

What's one point to a small team? Priceless. (Dennis Vogel)

Paul Stoddart and Zsolt Baumgartner. Not a plastic cup in sight. (Courtesy Sutton Motorsport Images)

Bruni: "For him, it was a joke, Formula 1, I think. For me, I was trying to have a job there and find a quicker drive. I'd been very quick in first qualifying and I was the only Minardi car who could

Minardi at Spa. (Courtesy Sutton Motorsport Images)

Following Ford's announcement in China and a disastrous Japanese Grand Prix, the finale in Brazil became the location of a party. A war party. Stoddart told *Autosport* 'the sport's fucked, our car's fucked. I don't want to go racing like this, everything's shit. All I want to do is go home.' To his eternal credit, he channelled his anger and achieved the nigh-impossible. All but Ferrari signed the 'Stoddart Declaration' agreeing to limit testing in 2005 and to go to a single tyre supplier. Not only that, but the nine signatories actually kept their word in 2005 and the FIA came to agree on the ridiculous amount of tyre testing. However, the isolation of Ferrari and Stoddart's bombastic style would have consequences. Jean Todt and Max Mosley wouldn't forget.

One of Stoddart's biggest supporters, Australian GP promoter and F1 Commission

challenge the Jordans. I beat Glock in first qualifying. We spoke and the guy who was quicker in first qualifying had the less fuel in second qualifying to try to beat the Jordan cars. Zsolt was last, I was 18th. This was agreed with the engineer ... Paul knew about everything and one minute before the session, he said Zsolt was going with no fuel. I said 'what's wrong?' Paul said he'd decided and if I didn't like it I didn't drive. This is what he said to me," laughs Bruni. "I was young but I wasn't stupid. I decided not to qualify the car because I didn't want to lose my time. He wanted Zsolt to be as quick as me because his sponsors were there. I know the reason, everybody knows the reason and Paul doesn't want to say it. Strange things happened [all year]. Even now I don't understand why he did certain things or changed his mentality with me. Honestly, I don't care anymore." Gimmi was the least of Stoddart's concerns at Interlagos.

Bruni at Spa-Francorchamps. Another unhappy race. (Courtesy Robert Murphy)

Have we got enough sponsors yet? (Courtesy Robert Murphy)

member Ron Walker, says Paul lost the plot. “He became a nuisance to Bernie and Max. Paul started to believe he was the representative of the teams or the champion of change. He came up against two seasoned operators that know fully well that people have come before them and haven’t succeeded and they were determined that Paul Stoddart would be part of the teams and not the chief agitator. Max today still helps the smaller teams because you need them to make up the complement in the paddock. Paul felt that he knew best and started to push his views too far.”

Stoddart says he was simply the mouthpiece. “I don’t think I was set up ... I was asked to be spokesman. Bernie didn’t want to promote it, he doesn’t do press conferences, Ian Phillips (of Jordan) felt it wasn’t his position, so muggins here was almost elected by default.”

The teams had been galvanised by FIA demands for a fax vote on the proposed changes which had been bubbling away all year. All the teams went straight into a meeting with Bernie. “The penny dropped that with Ford now out we’d been acting like a bunch of schoolchildren for too many years. We were effectively directors of Formula 1 and we’d been acting totally unprofessionally with people fighting their own corners. People really changed in that meeting. I still maintain what Max did was illegal.”

The teams would agree to some concessions like a single tyre supply and testing limit, but not V8 engines and new aerodynamic demands. "It was actually going to cost the small teams a small fortune. I already had a car for 2005, I had no money to build a second." This may be the truth but it is not the whole truth. Sources confirm Stoddart had a contingency plan.

Following a crash in practice by Michael Schumacher, Ferrari principal Jean Todt was in a team meeting and somehow didn't receive his invite to the second conference of team bosses. Paul Stoddart says it was a genuine misunderstanding which was to have corrosive consequences. "I later went with Bernie to his office with the agreement. He lashed out at Bernie with a verbal barrage of shit and it became clear that Todt felt he hadn't been invited to the meeting and things were being done behind his back. I thought they were going to throttle each other and I'm not exaggerating, I thought I was going to have to get in the middle of it. They were absolutely screaming at each other. That single non-invitation put the biggest divide between Ferrari and the rest of the teams because after that Todt was hostile to everything."

Ferrari is the only team with its own test track and the only team to build an extremely close relationship with a tyre supplier. Why would Maranello agree to limits on testing and an end to the tyre war? Why should it surrender its hard won advantages? Would McLaren or Williams if they were in the same situation? One doubts it. All this did lead to strange bedfellows, though. Defender of the independents, Max Mosley, was now allied to the grandest team of all. On the other side, the 'no-one ever helped us' brigade of Ron and Frank found themselves shoulder to shoulder with Paul.

Minardi crew at the inaugural Chinese Grand Prix. (Courtesy Sutton Motorsport Images)

2005

Smelling the espresso

"I'd gone in there with an olive branch but a couple of days later I found it was sticking out of my arse." Guess who.

Surely, it didn't have to end like this? Minardi now had two illegal cars and no money nor inclination to change them. Paul Stoddart set out on one last peace mission to his former ally Max Mosley. They met in London in January, and Stoddart says they were still getting on. "I said 'Max, why are you doing this? The teams are compromising. V8s are going to cost money, a testing cut is the way.' We had a very, very frank discussion but I did feel I'd gotten somewhere towards paving a solution, but I was wrong and this is where I saw the other side of Max. Our faxes were leaked [by the FIA]. Max Mosley will be remembered for being one of two people that made Formula 1 what it is today, but he is in clear danger of being remembered as the single person who tore it apart."

Hmm, that's not how it seemed during the middle of an enthralling 2007 season. Sure, there are no longer any plucky privateers and that's a shame, but did it have to be that way? Some of Stoddart's staunchest allies say he lost the plot entirely in early 2005.

"My time is now absolutely taken over by the politics. I'm seeing another side of Max and I am a loyal person. I know it doesn't sound like that because of the Ron and Frank thing but there's no malice in that. I cannot work out what happened to Max from May '04 onwards, he's a different Max. I believe passionately in Formula 1 and I believe what Max did is wrong. We have got the 2004 car [in Melbourne] and I have a verbal assurance from Max. I've even got a written assurance of a sort from Max saying that if we turn up with the '04 car for the first three races, provided we have agreement from all the teams, he can see no problem."

But Stoddart just knew it was going to be an interesting weekend. His cars did not conform to the new aerodynamic and safety specifications and so his lawyers were on standby. He was playing with fire here in, of all places, his home town.

"After chasing Todt down, who's now holding a grudge from what's happened at Brazil ... after a lot of to-ing and fro-ing on the Friday I get the signature to run the second session. I then see the stewards and Tony Scott Andrews ... I walk in there and I realise they've already been spoken to. Tony is a lawyer and no fool and he realised we'd done our homework and were fighting for a position of righteousness and he was put in a very painful position. We waited an hour or two while they deliberated ... I'd had a gutful of Max's politics and so had all the other teams. Minardi and six teams are together. Obviously, now Red Bull and Jordan are 'what the hell's going on here?' type of attitude. Ian Phillips reminded Colin Kolles there was a binding agreement and Christian Horner was reminded of Tony Purnell's agreement. So we get all ten signatures, see the stewards, they take my point but they say 'we are not adjudicators of Concorde, we are stewards of fact. Whilst you may have a case we don't feel we can intervene in any other way other than to deal with the written regulations and your car is not legal.'

"So I said 'I respect your position, I know why you've made it, I know who's made this decision.' I didn't make any secret of the fact I knew they were being told to say that. 'We have anticipated this and booked

Closed for business at the Australian Grand Prix. (Courtesy Sutton Motorsport Images)

His critics say Paul Stoddart enjoyed the media attention to the detriment of the team. (Courtesy Sutton Motorsport Images)

a session in the Victoria Supreme Court and I'm going to go there now for an emergency injunction. You're welcome to come with me if you want.' They said they didn't feel that was proper but they gave me their hotel room numbers."

Stoddart took the nuclear option and got his injunction against the stewards' decision. It's impossible to imagine Gian Carlo Minardi doing this and there remains much paddock scepticism about Stoddart's motives. Indeed, senior sources believe Minardi was entirely capable of taking two legal cars to Australia.

On Friday night, Paul and his lawyers had to issue subpoenas to all the team principals, to the stewards and to the FIA's race director Charlie Whiting. The good news was they were all in one place; the bad news was it was at Ron Walker's Grand Prix Ball for Melbourne high society at the Crowne Plaza.

"'I don't have time to have a shower, so rush from the court and get changed in the car into a mucky suit. Solicitors have gone off to prepare the affidavits, they say they'll meet me in the ball at 9 o'clock, can we issue them on the Friday night because it's for a hearing the next day at 2? I speak to the late John Large, who I've got great respect for, he was FIA vice president. He was a very sensible individual, not a political animal. I sat him down because I knew he had health problems. 'I have to give you some news but I don't want you to get stressed out because it's not personal against you.' He was fine about it, he said 'Paul, you know my hands are tied, I'd support you anyway I can but this will be Max's decision.'"

Even Stoddart wasn't enjoying this one, having to serve people with papers while they were enjoying themselves at a lavish party. Everyone knows what's going on but, keeping up appearances, pretending to ignore it. By now, the phone lines back to Max Mosley in Europe are glowing.

"Bugger me, just as I'm standing outside the door, Todt comes out and there are three girls getting autographs signed and I just couldn't resist it," laughs Stoddart. "I told the solicitors to get Todt's one out and I said 'go on, do it' and he walked over and served Todt, and it was the funniest thing I've ever seen because Todt started to sign it as a fucking autograph! He just said 'Mr Todt, you're served.' It was one of those classic moments and I'm standing ten feet away and Todt just gave me the evilest of all looks."

By now, Stoddart's mobile is also glowing and he ignores a summons to meet Ron Walker in his suite on the 21st floor. So Ron comes to fetch him.

"I walk in there and you've got Charlie and Herbie [Blash, also of the FIA] in their jeans, Richard Wood in his FIA kit, Alan Donnelly [Mosley's official representative], John Large, all of CAMS Australia, all of the Grand Prix senior management, lawyers introduced to me as representing the FIA, so you've got the lot. 21 people including myself. Bear in mind I've not had sleep now for two or three days, it's been really traumatic. Max was on the phone to John."

Ron Walker: "Not only was I upset but the government was upset because it put an enormous damper on the weekend. Even though certain teams represented themselves as followers of Paul, in the end, when Max and Bernie stepped in, it was the start of the end of Paul. At one stage we thought the race was going to be cancelled and we had sold millions of dollars worth of tickets. It was a very long Friday night that should have been a very pleasant night at a black tie ball where most of the leading players were huddled in a room with QCs trying to unscramble the eggs. I made a personal representation to Paul and told him this was bad for the sport, bad for Australia and we needed to back off and let the due [FIA] processes to take place. We were told in no uncertain terms that if he succeeded in the court, the race wouldn't come back to Australia."

Stoddart: "I was too tired to think straight. God, I'd love to live through that moment again because I agreed to back off. With hindsight, I wouldn't have and the history of Formula 1 would be different today. Max would have fallen there and then, he couldn't have survived. I believe categorically Max would have gone through with it and lost the presidency of the FIA. Hindsight is a wonderful thing but I should not have backed down. It's funny, because Max actually came clean at the last general meeting I did with all the principals (at Monza in September). It was one of the few times I spoke with him after Australia and he finally admitted 'while I don't agree with the way Paul went about Melbourne this year, he was actually right and had he gone through, we would have had to concede the regulations were indeed wrong.'"

Paul Stoddart insists it was a case of 'couldn't build legal cars' rather than 'wouldn't'. Finally, though, the exhausted, pressurised team principal gave in. Suddenly, everything was peace and light. 'How can we help you change the cars? What resources do you need?' Stoddart says if he'd stuck to his guns he would have got the court ruling on the Saturday. The consequence of that would have been that the two Minardi cars were the only legal ones in the pit lane. "That was being considered, don't you worry."

"We'd had parts flown out so we could do the rear wings, a few bits so we did the best we could and bastardised the car through the night. Basically, we ran a pile of shit. We were cutting bits off with carbon saws, just a joke.

"I was at the Australian Grand Prix in my own home town and I had people saying 'Paul, you're going to have the weight of responsibility of this being cancelled on your shoulders.' Had we been in any other country, including the UK, no fucking way would I have backed down. This has been said by many people more legal than me, that was perverting the course of justice, no ifs, no

He who giveth also taketh away. Bernie Ecclestone would once more engineer the sale of Minardi. (Courtesy Sutton Motorsport Images)

With those boys on your case, as Ron Walker observed, you are not going to win.

So was Stoddart intoxicated by his role of spokesman? Was he thinking straight? Surely, the cars could have been made legal before flying out to Australia? Why pick that fight? David and Goliath or death wish? Stoddart says he was mostly in control. "I don't think I was used by the teams; there is a slight truth but nobody made me say anything I didn't want to say. [Max] couldn't force me to sell the team, but you'd have to be pretty bloody thick not to realise your days are numbered."

Back in the pit lane, Minardi could now go racing. It was a similar last-gasp effort

buts. Mosley's blackmail was perverting the course of justice. He made himself above any law in any land." Strong stuff, strongly refuted by the FIA. It and its stewards have to enforce the rules and regulations. If a constructor chooses to turn up to a race with equipment it knows is ineligible, it knows the consequences.

The game was up. Bernie and Max let rip in the British press, realising they'd soon be rid of the Australian. Ecclestone used a gambling metaphor: "This is an expensive game to be sitting in on and if you can't afford the ante, you shouldn't take part in the school," he told *The Sun*. Bernie advised Paul Stoddart to take a leaf out of Eddie Jordan's book and sell soon. Bernie would find the buyer as he had in 1995 and 2001. Mosley later told *The Guardian*: "Stoddart is a sad case. I helped him tremendously when the other teams were trying to steal his money. But now my reaction is that he's obviously forgotten to take his medication."

A new car at last. Christijan Albers debuts the PS05 at Imola. (Courtesy Sutton Motorsport Images)

Gian Carlo Minardi with his assistant Roberta Leonardi at Minardi's final home race. (Robert Murphy)

to European Minardi's debut four years previously, but not quite so happy. Blow the politics, the two new drivers were just happy to be there. Since driving for Stoddart's F3000 team, Christijan Albers had won Germany's ultra-competitive and seriously quick touring car series, DTM. He was joined by Austria's Patrick Friesacher.

Dutchman Albers has no regrets about joining a team at the back of the F1 grid. "Not at all, because if you don't know any better, every F1 car you drive is the best in the world. A Minardi is still better than a DTM car, not that DTM is bad because it is a great competition. Formula 1 is Formula 1 and it's the nicest thing there is." There were two schools of thought on Minardi; drivers like Alonso and Webber loved it, Bruni and Verstappen emphatically did not. Albers says you have to hustle and make your own luck. "It's never sunshine everywhere, you have to create it yourself. You need a chance to get in a good team but to get this chance you have to create it. You have to give everything that you have. I had a really good school with HWA and Mercedes so I was quite well prepared when I came into F1."

The money situation in 2005 was shocking; title 'sponsor' was OzJet, Paul Stoddart's planned domestic airline for Australia. He was now clearly bankrolling the team until he got a better offer. Stoddart always maintained he would only sell to someone who could take the team forward and he was as good as his word.

A genuinely new car, the PS05, made its debut at the San Marino GP at Imola, Minardi's home race. It was an improvement but not enough to dominate the yellow cars of Jordan.

"It wasn't much quicker than the old car," says Albers. "Everyone was really motivated because it was the first new car in four years. We made progress and were challenging Jordan so it was nice to fight with somebody. The most important thing was the atmosphere was really good, we pushed really hard."

The race is remembered for Ferrari and Bridgestone coming good, Schumacher's monstering of Alonso in the closing laps and the Spaniard's fantastic defensive driving to take the win. He was on his way to the title and the baton had been passed at Imola – as it had been in tragic circumstances in 1994.

Imola 2005 also saw a marvellous celebration as Minardi fans from around the world converged on northern Italy. The 20th anniversary simply had to be marked and there were representatives from the US, the UK, Austria, the Republic of Ireland and, of course, Italy. A factory tour was organised by Minardi Club San Francisco and there was even a meal at La Tana del Lupo attended by the drivers, team officials, Gian Carlo Minardi and Pier Luigi Martini. Little did anyone realise it was, effectively, a last supper.

The high point of the season, and these things are relative, was a fantastic 15th place on the grid for Albers in Canada. "A lot of people came to me and said it was an amazing lap – all the laps I did were the same most of the time! Because of the low downforce level and the type of track Montreal is, the performance was much better from the car. We did a normal weekend but the results were much better because you can close things up. You also need to have a big heart because you arrive in turn five, the right hander that leads to another chicane, it was not really flat with the Minardi but I took it flat in qualifying; that was the difference between me and Friesacher. It was just a normal job like always but everyone saw us. And it wasn't down to low fuel, it was a good weekend."

A low point on the track had to be the use at a Grand Prix of 'test driver' Chanoch Nissany, a 42-year-old Israeli businessman with dreams of being an F1 driver. Apart from a wedge of the rolling stuff, dreams were all he had. On the Friday at the Hungaroring he was 12 seconds slower than his team-mates. "I don't care how slow he is, we needed budget to make the car quicker," insists Christijan. Fortunately, Nissany didn't kill himself or anyone else before he span, presumably out of good taste. The whole episode was a stain on the Minardi name and it even drew comment from Stoddart loyalist Mark Webber who branded it a 'joke'.

In a season when the tyre of choice was a Michelin, characteristically Minardi found itself on the other option. And tyres would provide Formula 1's nadir at the Indianapolis Motor Speedway. All the bitching, all the nonsense was brought to an

Patrick Friesacher in the PS05 at Imola. The new car was not the giant leap forward Minardi needed. (Courtesy Sutton Motorsport Images)

absolute boil when it became clear the Michelin teams couldn't race that particular circuit without blowing tyres. Others have dealt with the intricate details of this farce; suffice to say, Michelin was surprised with the track surface it encountered at Indy in 2005.

"It's quite easy," says Albers. "Two tyre companies are fighting for the championship and they are running on the edge, sometimes you go over it and that's what happened with the other side. If that happens, you have to sit on the side. It's not about safety at all, it's the risk you take. If the engine blows up you're not allowed to moan about it. That's the nicest thing about Formula 1, everything is to the limit."

A side-issue to most, but not this book, is why on earth did Minardi get involved? Paul Stoddart knew his contract with Bridgestone required him to race. It seems his attitude was 'I'm about to bail out, what the hell … lets get stuck in'. Maybe he couldn't stop himself. Yes, it was a joke race of just six cars but it still meant points for Minardi – maybe even a first and last podium.

On becoming FIA president in 1992, Max Mosley famously said Formula 1 ran itself and he wouldn't have to worry about it too much. This pleased the team principals who were thoroughly sick of Jean-Marie Balestre. The deaths of Ayrton Senna and Roland Ratzenberger in 1994 changed the landscape and Mosley is acclaimed for pushing through safety enhancements. Since then, he's worried about Formula 1 quite a bit. It just so happened in 2005 he attended neither the Australian nor the US Grands Prix. Both key showdowns were via fax, phone and proxy. The threat

Minardi club at Mirabeau: Albers practicing ahead of Trulli, Alonso and Webber. (Courtesy Sutton Motorsport Images)

of cancelling Indianapolis came as no surprise to Paul Stoddart, as he'd experienced 'remote control' Max three months earlier in Melbourne; Max "at his absolute worst," and, if you believe the team principals, at some odds with the FIA president who publicly talks of not interfering with the FIA's stewards and officials.

Jean Todt of Ferrari quite rightly said it wasn't his problem. Neither would he agree to the proposal for a chicane. The Michelin teams along with David Coulthard, Indy 500 winner Gil de Ferran of Honda and Paul Stoddart wanted to slow down the Michelin cars on the banking, let the Bridgestone cars run high, only let the Bridgestone teams score points, whatever – just put on a show. They were even prepared to run a non-championship race if Mosley cancelled the Grand Prix. The chicane was the same solution approved by Mosley's FIA at Barcelona after the crashes at Imola in 1994.

"Max gets poor old Burdette Martin [American FIA delegate] on the phone, another elderly guy and absolutely drums him into the ground 'if this happens, if you guys do this, I will ban all motorsport in North America. The leopard never changes his spots. The teams were going to fucking do it, fuck Max. If he had cancelled that Grand Prix, I promise you nine teams were going to compete." Stoddart says team principals were aghast, saying Max had no idea how serious the situation was.

Former lawyer Max Mosley refused to allow the chicane and,

cleverly, he also refused to cancel the race, leaving the ball in the teams' court. Michelin couldn't guarantee tyre safety to its customers in the most litigious country in the world, and that was that.

"Colin Kolles [Jordan] broke the mould, if it wasn't for him we wouldn't have run. They were our only competitors that year. We were all sat in Bernie's office and Sam Michael [Williams] and myself were the only two with radios and we heard 'car going down the pit lane'. Sam said 'who is it?' and we just expected it to be Rubens or Michael and they said 'it's Narain'," Stoddart laughs. "We looked around the room and it was only then we realised Kolles wasn't there. We had [Indianapolis owner] Tony George there, head in hands, close to tears, saying 'what's he going to do? They're going to

Albers practised in sunshine at Indianapolis, but storm clouds were gathering. (Courtesy Robert Murphy)

A furious Indy crowd watches the Bridgestone Six start its 'race'. (Courtesy Sutton Motorsport Images)

tear his place apart.' Bernie really agitated. Flavio so fucking upset he threw his phone across the room. Ron fuming. Poor old Pierre [Dupasquier of Michelin] absolutely beside himself."

The Michelin teams only took to the grid for Bernie, who was contractually obliged to provide the promoter and broadcasters with 20 cars on the grid itself. After the parade lap, they all came into the pits leaving two Ferraris, two Jordans and two Minardis. The Indy crowd erupted.

"I saw a broken Bernie," says Stoddart. "If it wasn't for loyalty to Bernie, none of those cars would've gone out so the grid could be formed and Bernie had fulfilled his obligations."

Before and during the 'race', Stoddart was telling anyone who'd listen that if both Jordans broke down he would call in his cars. He denies any embarrassment that, even now, Minardi couldn't get on the podium. Former Minardi test driver Tiago Monteiro took third for Jordan. "I couldn't get past him in the race because I had problems with the gearbox," says Albers. "I was happy to finish the race in front of Patrick because he didn't have any problems and if he'd finished the year with one point more than me it would be unbearable! Of course it was a race, I was racing Patrick all year because there was nobody else to race. I'm a racing driver, quite an ego and I don't give a shit about others. That's how you have to be."

Minardi mechanic Matt Goodwin with an in-joke aimed at 'Visa' watching the TV at home. (Courtesy Sutton Motorsport Images)

In the paddock, the game was up. Not just for Minardi but Sauber and Jordan too. Engine deals were far too costly and the cut of the F1 revenue unfair. Eddie Jordan cashed-in his chips after years of criticising manufacturer dominance and the remaining privateers weighed up their options. Both Peter Sauber and Paul Stoddart found they agreed with Eddie. Sauber sold out to BMW and by September Stoddart had agreed a deal with Red Bull. He claims to have received more than 40 approaches during his five years at the helm.

In September 2004, he confirms there was a $50m bid from Dutch firm Spyker, which later bought Jordan/Midland for more than double. "Perhaps there was a better deal to be done for Minardi there," he concedes.

In 2005, a Russian bid, fronted by former Ferrari driver Eddie Irvine, came very close before being trumped by Red Bull. Stoddart says the Russian deal was his 39th offer and "they were bloody close, Eddie would tell you he thought he'd done the deal." Stoddart had to exclude Irvine while Red Bull carried out its due diligence. "In fact, they'd been told to buy it. I can't prove it." Stoddart decided this was the one – a company which could advance the team and keep it operating out of Faenza, for the time being. He says Red Bull paid $35m and assumed a debt of $14m.

Minardi himself denies yet another rumoured Italian consortium was a serious prospect, "There were some people but mentioning them is useless. A group of

Robert Doornbos about to be lapped by Alonso at the Hungaroring. He had replaced Patrick Friesacher. (Courtesy Sutton Motorsport Images)

Albers qualified an excellent 15th but withdrew from the inaugural Turkish Grand Prix. (Courtesy Sutton Motorsport Images)

entrepreneurs, a lot of talk and little action, certainly not a lot of money." The same old story.

Announcing the sale, Stoddart paid tribute to his staff: "I'm proud of each and every member of the Minardi team. Together with all of our colleagues back at the factory in Faenza, this team has a heart and soul second to none. The words, 'Never has so much been achieved by so few with so little,' can never have been as justified as they are with Minardi. Given that the team has survived against all odds over the years, competing with both dignity and passion while contributing so much to the FIA Formula 1 World Championship, today is a sad day. I would also like to express my sincere gratitude to our engine partner, Cosworth, to our commercial and technical partners, and to the thousands of Minardi fans around the world, for their unconditional support of the hard-trying little team from Faenza over the years. Finally, I want to thank Gian Carlo Minardi. Unless he had possessed the vision and the bravery to strike out into Formula 1 in the first place, and the resilience to deal with the innumerable problems and difficulties that arose along the way, the team would undoubtedly have suffered the same fate as many well-known, and frequently better funded organisations, and simply fallen by the wayside. Regrettably, the Minardi name will now disappear from the sport, but I firmly believe the competitive spirit that has burned brightly within this team for the past 21 years will live on under its new owners."

The 2005 Chinese Grand Prix was the 750th in the history of the Formula 1 World Championship. It was Minardi's 340th

One of Minardi's passions is finding new talent. (Courtesy Sutton Motorsport Images)

and last. For the record, Robert Doornbos finishing 14th was a marginal improvement on Minardi's first race in Brazil in 1985 when Pier Luigi Martini made the first of many retirements. Both Cosworth-powered cars, by the way, had qualified last.

The tributes rolled in:

"I think it's very sad that Minardi won't be there." Nigel Mansell.

"It is not the power of money that gives them their fighting spirit, it is the power of the people. They were a good thing for F1: now, it is often all about business, but with Minardi, everything was just about motor racing." Fernando Alonso.

"It's sad but I'm afraid it was inevitable – it isn't a sport anymore, it's now just big business. Motorsport isn't there, motor business is." Sir Stirling Moss.

"I am very sad to see them go. My first test was there, my first F1 race too, and I have to say thank you to Gian Carlo Minardi for the opportunity. The atmosphere was fantastic, with the Italian mechanics, and we laughed all the time. It is a great team, and they will always have a place in my heart." Giancarlo Fisichella.

"It is sad but things change. When you talk about Minardi, you have to remember teams like Lotus are no longer around so it happens to the best teams. To survive in F1 takes an extraordinary amount of dedication and talent and unfortunately Minardi dropped off the bottom. Sad to see them go, they were much loved, people knew they were trying and they had a good spirit about them and that is a key part of the appeal of the sport." Damon Hill.

"Through 9/11, through bloody sponsors

Red Bull deal on the horizon at Spa-Francorchamps. (Courtesy Sutton Motorsport Images)

Minardi gives Albers the thumbs up. He is flanked by two mechanics who were there in Brazil 1985: Manucci (holding helmet) and Zama (wearing white gloves). (Courtesy Sutton Motorsport Images)

Double Dutch at Minardi's final Grand Prix. Doornbos leads Albers. (Courtesy Sutton Motorsport Images)

Doornbos would later win for Minardi Team USA in Champ Cars. (Courtesy Sutton Motorsport Images)

who didn't pay, I kept the team going against all odds and I passed it on to a safe pair of hands," says Stoddart. "When I left Minardi it was in a far better shape than the day I came in. I exited with about the same money as I entered, a reasonable break-even position. I was certainly more worldly-wise. Throughout that five years I gave an honest account of myself, I didn't take bullshit and roll over and lay down, I fought for what I believed in and believed in what I fought in."

They may be compatriots, but F1 Commission member Ron Walker is about as different from the anti-establishment Paul Stoddart as you can get. Yet Walker admits there is an irony in wanting an underdog as long as it doesn't bark too loudly. "Correct, and Paul wanted a greater share of the TV money, he wanted a bigger slice of the action for the Jordans of life and the others who weren't faring too well, and he probably believed at the time that there was too much advantage to the Ferraris and the Williams and the McLarens. What he forgot was not so many years ago Ferrari was the underdog, and before that Williams was. They've all been through the cycle of disappointment." So if Stoddart had towed the line, he could still be around? "Paul didn't learn politics quick enough. The politics in the paddock is something to be mastered and Paul was a slow learner in terms of understanding the politics of Formula 1. It plays a big part. He'd still be there and he'd be making a fortune, the way the other teams are now because everything's been realigned financially."

Paul Stoddart: "That is true but with caveats. Paul learned the politics of Formula 1 the hard way. First I had to deal with Prost, then I had to deal with Walkinshaw, then I had to deal with fighting funds, then I had to deal with engine supply and so on and so forth. Did I take on too much? Absolutely. Did I get out at the right time? There's an argument I didn't but it's never wrong to take a profit and then look where Jordan is today. The one thing that hasn't

The final team photo in Shanghai; sixty people compared to the thirteen in Rio 1985. (Courtesy Sutton Motorsport Images)

Heart and soul. (Courtesy Sutton Motorsport Images)

changed is that only the top ten teams get paid and if I was there as team eleven or twelve, Minardi would've gone down. So Ron is right, in a ten team championship or twelve teams all getting paid championship, which it is not, then he is right I shouldn't have sold, I should have backed off a little bit and rode the waves but that option didn't exist. I was sick of trying to fight for twelve teams being paid. Certain team principals were never going to give on that and so I felt it was the right time to go." Stoddart was speaking before the 2007 agreement among the small teams to share their spoils.

Despite a petition of 15,000 Minardi fans, organised by forzaminardi.com, there was no way 'Minardi' would be included in the new name, as BMW had done with Sauber. Red Bull simply wanted to run four cars under its banner but when it was denied it reverted to Scuderia Toro Rosso, Italian for 'Team Red Bull'. Rather than Eddie Irvine, it was another Maranello old boy who bought into the project, Gerhard Berger. By December, even Gian Carlo Minardi was out.

"I know that I've been criticised heavily by the fans," says Stoddart, more in sadness than in anger. "All I can say to them is if they were in possession of all the facts they would understand Minardi would have closed five years earlier and it would have been a total closure, everybody would have lost their jobs and no resemblance to it would ever have existed from that day forward. At least it had a dignified transition to Red Bull and I'm proud to say that most of the people and the facility live on in Faenza."

Throughout its remarkable run in Formula 1, Minardi had enjoyed and endured a curious relationship with Ferrari. Would

Jean Todt miss his opposite number at Minardi? “No,” said the top man at Maranello, who wasn’t going to even attempt to be magnanimous. “Stoddart has not given anything to Formula 1.” That, of course, is petulant nonsense. Without Stoddart, Minardi would have died five years earlier. There would have been no prep school for Alonso, no Albert Park ’02, no Indianapolis ’04. No-one with the gumption to stand-up to the big boys who were spending F1 into oblivion and who, in the end, found they agreed with Paul Stoddart. Peter Sauber didn’t do that. Eddie Jordan certainly didn’t, even when he had a golden opportunity.

F1 without Stoddart is less fun and less honest.

Epilogue

The 2005 Chinese Grand Prix wasn't quite the last run for the Minardi F1 team. Days before the handover to Red Bull, the final 'test' session came at Rome's Vallelunga circuit, with both Gian Carlo and Paul honouring some outstanding commitments. Roldan Rodriguez drove the F1 car and would later sign for the Minardi-Piquet Sports GP2 team. Also testing at Vallelunga was Davide Rigon, who would drive for the Minardi F3000 team, and Katherine Legge, becoming the first woman in years to test an F1 car. Paul Stoddart had the honour of driving the last laps in the PS05 and said "It turned out a more emotional experience than I expected it to be." He then threw a party for the team at Faenza's Cavallino hotel, where it had all begun for him almost five, frantic years earlier.

"Unlike me, Stoddart turned this operation into a business," says Gian Carlo Minardi. "His abilities were helped by the bad luck and misfortunes of others [Prost and Arrows]. There were ten teams left so he had to be helped to stay in the championship. They accepted his attacks or his battles. This situation allowed him to survive with very little money (other teams would spend in one month what we spent in a year). He didn't make investments, he didn't do what Minardi first and Rumi later did."

Minardi told *Autosport* magazine "We have managed to save all the workforce. If the price to pay was [losing] the name, then never mind. But don't think I'm happy about it. I didn't follow the advice I was given by a man with whom I had a relationship in the early seventies, long before getting into F1. That man told me: 'Minardi, sell your stock, sell whatever you want, but don't ever sell your name.' That man's name was Enzo Ferrari. Instead [of selling it] I gave the name away for free. I'm left with the satisfaction of having built a company where in 21 years there have been 380 employees. There are teams that use more personnel in a single GP. Among them there are people who saw with me the first and the last GP, so I'm proud of this fact. We missed the results, the joy of a podium. There remains the good and the bad choices, like having gifted the shares of the teams to Stoddart in order to let Minardi survive. And now Stoddart has sold them, lucky him. But I prefer to have the team in Faenza rather than to read my name over a factory in England."

Gian Carlo obviously has mixed feelings about Stoddart's very un-Minardi way of operating, but then, Gian Carlo hadn't actually owned the team since 1993. By 2005, Minardi was the fourth oldest constructor in the World Championship, so was he upset to finally see his name disappear? "I don't want to get into this. Who made this decision [Dietrich Mateschitz of Red Bull] had the right to do it. I honestly wish him to reach the goals that Gian Carlo Minardi wasn't able to reach."

In 2007, Paul Stoddart launched Minardi Team USA in Champ Cars, and he's sanguine about Gian Carlo's feelings. "Knowing Gian Carlo and how emotional he is, I don't take issue with his comments on selling the name. The reality is when I bought the team I bought the name. The fact I used it in several entities was with Gian Carlo's blessing. You don't think anyone's going to change it, it was just one of those things. So much of me is in Minardi and we continue to operate the two seaters under Minardi anyway. I only sold the Italian company and I retained the rights to the name so it was a logical progression for me to continue with Minardi. I'm proud of Minardi; I'm proud of what Gian Carlo did and I'm proud of what I did so I don't see the need to have 'Stoddart Racing'. We have joint rights. He has the logo, the yellow and blue colours and Minardi in Italy. Probably arguable in Europe, certainly not in the UK but we are fine about this. I had several companies registered as Minardi and I only sold one of them. I probably could have objected about his new teams [in F3000 and GP2] but what for? I have all the time in the world for the guy and I wish him all the very best so I'm hardly going to stand in the way of the guy using his own name."

There's no doubt it was an odd relationship. Gian Carlo wanted to hang around, protect 'his people' at Faenza, do a bit of talent-spotting, help with sponsorship, stay busy. Paul liked him and couldn't face kicking the guy out. It was Gian Carlo's life.

British mechanic Matt Goodwin says everyone found it a little strange. "I think it was a difficult arrangement really, probably more so for Paul with him not being at the factory. The Italians seemed to listen to Gian Carlo when he was there and then ignore him when Paul was at the factory. Paul was always the boss but I don't think Minardi's influence was always positive. During the race he was more of a co-ordinator. He could speak English but he chose not to. I think he had a lot of mistrust for the English. He hung around probably because it was his baby, it was his name above the door and he wasn't exactly flooded with job offers, I imagine."

September 11th 2001 had all sorts of implications and in the grand scheme of things motorsport is way down the list. However, it did hit sponsorship generally and Paul Stoddart in particular, as his 'day job' is European Aviation. Nevertheless, Minardi slates Stoddart for cutting back research and development, testing and racing the same monocoque for three years. Stoddart hesitates before responding: "Knowing Gian Carlo as I do, it is close to the truth. I wouldn't quite describe it like that because I took the riskiest decision in my life to buy into something I didn't really know and I kept them all going. Yes, in 2002, '03 and '04 we did race with the same monocoque because of sponsors like Gazprom, and half the money from Malaysia defaulted. We never had the money to do anything else. Had it been an 11 team championship we would have been in trouble. Plus September 11th destroyed my business. Gian Carlo puts it in his own little style. I don't disagree with that but I wouldn't use the word 'gifted'. People might have a different opinion if they'd been through it," he laughs.

"He has mixed emotions but the real issue here is through God knows how many owners and how many deals, Gian Carlo did actually manage to survive all those years and, although I broke my neck and really went out on a limb to keep him in the team, when it was sold (and there's no doubt the Red Bull deal was the right thing to do; if you go back there today 75 per cent of the faces are the same people and it's in the same place and they're talking about building a new factory in Faenza) I really went to great lengths to keep the senior people there. Sadly, for one reason or another, certain people just didn't cut it with the new management and they're gone."

There's one constant under Minardi, Rumi and Stoddart – sponsorship fouled up time after time. "Defaulting is in motorsport, full stop," says Stoddart. "People make commitments on the hype and everything's great and beautiful and then they realise they're paying a lot of money for their sign on the side of a car. This is not just Formula 1. You get a lot of dreamers who fall in love with the limelight but the reality is they haven't got the money to do it. You do get a lot of chancers, I had an absolute bloody entourage turn up to buy Minardi over the years. I used to joke Red Bull were number 37 and by the time I sold they were 41! I've got a €10m bounced cheque in my drawer from one arsehole. When you're that end of the grid, your percentage of arseholes and non-payers is high. I was so sick of Stayer in 2004 in Japan I put a sticker over their logo saying 'did not pay'."

Knowing what he knows now, Stoddart has a similar critique of Minardi.

"He never had the manufacturer involvement and he never had the level of sponsorship that was needed to run a Formula 1 team in the modern era. Was that his fault? No, he just didn't get the breaks. BAR could easily have bought him but they would have shut him down in 1997 as they did with Tyrrell. Rumi was the right move at the time but he didn't have deep enough pockets. Minardi is littered with stories where it's on the brink of success. PSN deal? Didn't happen. Gazprom deal? $50m; didn't happen. They've all been there but Gian Carlo never managed to get one over the wire and that's why the team suffered. Given the budget I did have it did a fantastic job."

Fernando Alonso and Mark Webber agree: "I feel sorry for them now because it was a fantastic team," says Alonso. "They are fantastic people but I guess most of them are working at Scuderia Toro Rosso (STR) so I feel happy for the boys. For sure, we will miss Minardi, even if it's the smallest team, never got the results, the name of Minardi is famous in Formula 1 after 20 years and we will miss them."

"Stoddie had F1 worked out pretty quickly in terms of what you're up against," says his compatriot Webber. "Eddie Jordan was probably the last guy to make it work with Frentzen in '99. Stoddie knew the strong guys get stronger and the weaker guys do struggle to make progress unless you can get a good leg-up somewhere along the line. He tried his best and I've got friends for life there, in terms of the guys who worked on my car. I know all of them. Paul was very special to me because of the opportunity he gave to me and Mr Minardi, I feel I have a special relationship with the Italians because of what happened to me. Very fond memories, they would walk over hot coals those guys. It was the slowest car but if we stopped in testing they would run the length of the pit lane, they would get the car back there, they would work on it. I tell you what, some other teams could learn from that. Minardi did things special."

But there are some detractors and some of those will go on the record. Alex Yoong: "He bought a couple of jumbo jets when I was there, he bought five I believe," laughs Alex. "My budget didn't all go into the race team. Paul is a battler and a scraper and he kept Minardi afloat using his own money or whatever but he was very bad for Minardi. He wasn't a racing man so he made some strange decisions and the way he went about things was, in the long run, very bad for Minardi. It would never, ever have improved with Paul there. Paul selling it was the best thing that ever happened to Minardi. Paul did the best that he could by his own standards. He never knowingly tried to do the wrong thing. He's been a battler, a scraper his whole life, taking risks and doing strange things to get what he wants. To run a team, to make progress, to have a future, he didn't know what he was doing. Minardi is Gian Carlo. Paul would make promises to people. Some guys had to stay with the team purely to get the money Paul owed them. I'm really happy to see the guys happy now with STR and they have a chance to fight."

More in hope than expectation, Paul Stoddart applied for an FIA Formula 1 entry under the new regulations for 2008. They allowed 'junior' teams to buy cars from established players but, unsurprisingly, Stoddart's bid was unsuccessful. The place went to former BAR boss David Richards.

Despite their differences, Australian GP promoter and member of the F1 Commission Ron Walker says Stoddart could still be in the big time, if he'd played his cards right. "He should be in Formula 1 today because he provides enormous colour to the sport and they need colourful people in the pit lane. He was a great friend of the journalists, they loved him, they loved to print what he said but, alas, it's very sad he's not there. Bernie went out of his way to support Paul financially, advancing him money to keep him going."

"Paul was not in racing all that long," says Eddie Jordan. "I had 35 years in racing; I'd seen some tragic sides and I'd seen some glorious sides. Paul was caught up in [the politics], I think he probably paid too much attention to the media who were using him, perhaps."

Paul Stoddart occasionally betrays some regret at how he played his cards. It does seem odd how he rapidly switched from Mosley ally to anti-Mosley cheerleader. There was certainly little love lost with Ferrari principal Jean Todt, who went out of his way to flick his fingers at Stoddart on Minardi's departure. But forget the personalities, Ferrari has always cast a giant shadow over Minardi. Gian Carlo thought it could be a benign 'Big Brother', but it was rather more Orwellian than that.

"It's a Ferrari-dependent country, with all due respect for that team and what they've won, the Italian press is conditioned. Many important things we have done were barely noticed," says Minardi.

"There's only one team, Ferrari," says Italian driver Gimmi Bruni. "All the rest is nothing. Even Minardi with his experience and good new names in F1, even that was not enough. Italian people don't care about motorsport at all, they just care about Ferrari."

"Ferrari is Ferrari, Minardi is Minardi," concedes Gian Carlo. "It is not useful to think about 'what would have happened if?' You don't make history with 'if'. They follow other roads to victory, so we cannot criticise them. We go on, our way."[1]

Well, you can try. From the very start to the bitter end, Minardi just couldn't get out of the shadow cast by 'The Other Italian Team'. Even when Maranello wasn't actively meddling, corporate Italy's love affair with Ferrari meant it was very hard for Gian Carlo to find sponsors.

Forget Ferrari, forget money, forget the language barrier; it's often said by Minardi's friends that he's simply too nice for Formula 1. Maybe that's getting near the truth.

Bernie Ecclestone: "The good thing about Gian Carlo is he was very well liked and respected throughout the paddock. I never heard anybody say anything bad about him, which is good. I suppose he would think language was a problem. He's not an outgoing guy like Stoddart so if he'd have spoken English, I don't know how it would have helped him. He had a lot of friends and associates who had a lot of respect for him."

Jaime Manca-Graziadei: "People had too much access. He was too nice and in F1 you don't get anywhere like that. He knows it but he's proud of it because he's an honest, loyal person which is what people ought to be. His other problem is he hates the English, he doesn't understand them and he wouldn't learn the language of F1. He is rooted to Faenza. I used to pull his leg all the time – we would drive out of Faenza and when we got to the next village, Castel Bolognese, I would say 'Gian Carlo, if they stop us you'd better let me speak because you don't speak the fucking language!' It was a joke between me and him and we still joke about it. The only English word he knew was 'white' because it was the nickname he gave me for my hair."

Mechanic Luca Zama was at Rio '85 and was there at the end. "Gian Carlo for me is firstly a good friend. He's different from other team bosses. The problem is he can be too passionate. His language is not so technical. I think in some decisions he trusted some engineers too much! But F1 needs more passion. Now the system is too much like a robot."[2]

Aldo Costa agrees with the 'too nice' analysis. "One of his problems was he didn't want to be more international and he stayed too focussed on Italy and Faenza. It was good at the beginning but then when Formula 1 started to grow from a couple of million Euros for an engine supply, it became very expensive. By the mid-90s it was almost impossible."

Despite everything, despite all the grief, despite the hand-to-mouth existence, Gian Carlo Minardi had stayed loyal to his people at Faenza and they had stayed loyal to him, including five staff from that very first race in 1985. He opened the factory each and every morning and he continued to help with sponsorship and talent-spotting. It was a sad, fizzle-out end to his days at No 21 Via Spallanzani. No more Minardi Team SpA.

"There is a lot of love towards the people still working there, 80 per cent maybe wouldn't have been in Formula 1 without Minardi in Faenza. Please allow me to be proud of this. I've been with the team for many years and therefore I will watch what they do with keen interest. I will be impartial, because I won't discuss Red Bull's decisions. I will be a fan who will watch the World Championship with interest.

"Over the years, we have experienced a number of problems, but we've been able to deal with them thanks to the passion that has always existed within this team. I want to thank all the guys, at the races and at the factory, for the effort they have put in over these last 21 years. I also want to thank all the drivers, who have helped to make this team great, and all the sponsors and fans, who have supported us unstintingly."

He was never going to be another Enzo. Even his own staff say he was too nice for the piranha club. His fundamental failure was the inability to secure a decent, sustained engine supply at any point in Minardi history. Poor luck is involved but, more than that, it was a structural failure of the team. Those less kind would point to a lack of ambition or even incompetence. This writer believes that unfair. Williams and Tyrrell made their own luck and capitalised – but they are in the minority.

He started as an F1 talent spotter and ended as one and that's where one senses he's happiest – at a karting track or F3 race, making notes. "I like to see minor races. That's where you find drivers. I like to trust people and not only those who win." If only he'd taken a cut from the future contracts of those he's signed. "I was talking with some friends the other evening: if I had asked two per cent flat from everyone, they would have all accepted because it's a ridiculous amount of money and today I would be retired." Yet it's also important to put into context the tag of 'talent-spotting genius'. During the Fisichella, Trulli, Alonso and Webber era it was much more a collaborative effort, not least because Minardi no longer owned the team. Flavio Briatore was very much in the driving seat, even after he sold his stock. Also, the memory is a wonderful, rose-tinted thing. One tends to remember the successes while the amount of cash a driver brings will often mean more than the amount of talent. For every Alonso there's a Yoong; for every Martini, a Mazzacane.

Most new teams struggle, struggle a bit more, then fold. Look at the list of those that fell by the wayside during Minardi's time in F1:

AGS
Alfa Romeo
Arrows
Brabham
Coloni
Dallara
Forti
Jaguar
Lamborghini
Larrousse
Ligier/Prost
Lola
Lotus
March
Onyx
Osella
Pacific
RAM
Rial
Simtek
Spirit
Toleman
Tyrrell
Zakspeed

Staying in Formula 1 is not easy, so Minardi's remarkable story is one of survival – a success in itself. Somehow it paid the bills and kept the show on the road for 21 years. Motorsport fans should thank Gian Carlo Minardi. A good man who helped keep F1 real, kept it smiling, kept it human. And he kept on spotting great drivers.

His team holds a record which will (probably) never be broken – 340 Grands Prix without a pole position, and it's second only to Arrows in number of races without a win (Arrows contested 382). The tally in the Grand Prix Data Book reads:

Starts 634
Points 38
Poles –
Fastest laps –
Wins –

The statistics are the truth. But they're nowhere near the whole truth.

[1] Interview with Minardi Club San Francisco
[2] *Autosport* 31.3.2005

Postscript

What did you expect? He can't stay away from motor racing circuits, never could. Ironic, too, that the track which has given him so much joy is neither Imola, nor Monza, but Silverstone; the very lair of Ron and Frank. On Sunday, 13th August 2006, less than a year after the demise of Minardi F1, Minardi won its first race in a quarter of a century. Roldan Rodriguez added his name to that of Michele Alboreto in the rather select club of Minardi winners. Gian Carlo Minardi had given his name, know-how and livery to an F3000 Euroseries team run by his son Giovanni. Fans around the world hoped this was the start of a campaign to get back to Formula 1, but don't hold your breath. "I believe it is impossible today," laments Gian Carlo. "It's a chapter which has come to an end. You need financial resources which are not available in Italy. It's a Ferrari-dependent country."

F2 became F3000 which eventually became GP2, and in 2007, Minardi would compete in the series as Minardi Piquet Sports. Other team owners in GP2 included Adrian Campos and Giancarlo Fisichella.

On the other side of the Atlantic, in a completely separate operation, Paul Stoddart was launching Minardi Team USA in Champ Cars. 2003 Minardi driver Justin Wilson was already there, driving for a rival team. "I think it's great. It's a shame he couldn't continue in Formula 1 but times change and it's good to have the Minardi name back racing at this level and to have Paul over here. I think he's a great guy and I have a lot of respect for him." Robert Doornbos, who drove for Minardi in its last Formula 1 Grand Prix in China, won at Mont Tremblant, so joining the Minardi winners' club. The very first SMS text message congratulating Paul Stoddart came from Gian Carlo.

And, in a parallel universe, there is still a Minardi F1 car racing, and it's doing rather well. Rodrigo Gallego drives the venerable M185 in the FIA Historic Formula 1 Championship. "Gian Carlo Minardi has given us huge support. The biggest problem was the aerodynamics because it was built for a turbo and with our 550bhp Cosworth we had serious problems in a straight line."

Despite the teething trouble [still!] Rodrigo won his category in 2005 and was able to get within two seconds of the Brabham BT49 ground effect car.

"[The Minardi] is a well constructed car. It has got a lot of attention and admiration because people are not used to seeing a Minardi racing at the front. We won in 2006 so it's Minardi's first FIA championship title."

In the FIA Formula 1 World Championship, the 'ten team' issue came to a head as the last 'independent', Spyker (nee Midland, nee Jordan), threatened to sue the team formerly known as Minardi. Spyker was bound to finish 11th and, in July 2007, reached an agreement with the customer teams Scuderia Toro Rosso and Super Aguri to share the funds due to the teams which finished 9th and 10th. It was a neat, inevitable agreement which may well have been brokered by Bernie Ecclestone. Paul Stoddart could probably have been part of it had he hung around long enough, but his goose had been cooked on a Melbourne barbecue back in 2005.

Mind you, in a remarkable turn up for the books, Minardi did sort of make the Albert Park grid in 2006. Super Aguri only raced thanks to some four-year-old cars bought by Paul Stoddart in the Arrows 'fire auction'. One of them, painted in Minardi colours, had been on display outside McDonald's in Melbourne Airport. "Super Aguri did a good job in '06 but then they had a lot of help," says Stoddart. "I gave them a chassis which was at Tullamarine airport. It's got to be the funniest story of all time. January 2006 it was sitting outside McDonald's with kids climbing all over it and that very car was racing in Melbourne two months later!"

As Bernie would say: 'Typical Minardi.'

Minardi fans

On one thing, Gian Carlo Minardi and Paul Stoddart readily agree. Minardi fans are a bit special. They're hardly 'glory chasers' in the traditional sense. They understand there's much more pleasure to be had in battling for a point here and a point there. It's an exclusive and friendly club. "I want to thank all the fans, who have supported us unstintingly," says Minardi. Stoddart admits he was amazed by the strength and depth of the fan-base. "Montreal and San Francisco are the two clubs which stand out, the two most active which I've had the privilege of working with. I was surprised [by it] when I started with Minardi, we also built it up in Australia."

Through the good offices of forzaminardi.com, here's a selection of memories:

"When they entered F1, Minardi were awful. But they kept going. They got better. And better. They became a team who clearly had both passion and technical creativity, and for whom racing was about the racing. They were indescribably cool. They did tend to break your heart once a fortnight, but that simply made the triumphs sweeter."
Marcus Hassall, Brigg, UK [aka silverghost]

"Supporting Minardi was pretty weird, that's for sure. In Italy, when Ferrari is something like the national football team, it is a credo, there's no room for anything else. It also worked like that for me. I did love Ferrari. Michele Alboreto first, when I was a boy. What a man, and a driver. And then 'my' Jean Alesi, Sicilian like me, he was my idol. The last 'romantic' Formula 1 driver. Then, something changed. Ferrari started to win, but at the same time, it became something different. Minardi had always been my second team. I remember perfectly the first time they got two cars in the points, GCM jumping for joy, it was great. It happened naturally. I started to follow the Faenza underdog more and more. The less I cared for Ferrari, the more I cared for Minardi. Seeing Luca Badoer crying in Nürburgring switched on something in my tifosi heart. Then came Alonso and, after, that night pushing Mark Webber from my sofa, crazy for joy for that great fifth place in Australia. People laughed sometimes about that. It made me like it more. It's nice to feel unique. That was Minardi. It was a little world of loyal, romantic people I discovered on the web. It was a mood, a way of being different. And special."
Salvatore Toscano, Palermo, Italy [salvo]

Pier Luigi Martini with two of his many fans. (Courtesy Robert Murphy)

Minardi Club San Francisco organised a 20th birthday party for Minardi at Faenza's finest eatery, La Tana del Lupo. (Courtesy Robert Murphy)

"One Gian Carlo Minardi is worth 100 Ron Dennises any day. The Minardi F1 team reminded me what I loved about F1 when I first got into it back in the early 1970s ... when it was still a sport. How can you keep going for years with no financial resources or convincing results in a sporting discipline as elitist as Formula 1 without being tempted just to let it all go? As Gian Carlo would say, "for the love of racing." The Faenza boys raced to race. Gian Carlo attempts to have a pure Italian team in 1985 and goes with Carlo Chiti and his Motori Moderni. For three years he is loyal, then he goes with a Cosworth DFZ and has some success. If you really look at the Minardi story, there is the recurring theme. Minardi is so close to turning the corner but something or somebody or just simply fate thwarts their effort in one way or another. But look at the young drivers that have come through Faenza; Nannini, Martini, Fisichella, Trulli, Alonso. Designers and managers such as Aldo Costa, Gustav Brunner and Nigel Cowperthwaite. The clincher for me is this; Gian Carlo Minardi was not in this to make money, all monies earned were ploughed back into the team. Gian Carlo made deals to save the team more than once, the team was more important to him than anything else."

Robert Murphy, Elizabeth, Pennsylvania, USA [Murph]

Minardi fans at Imola 2005, including: Salvatore Toscano (front, draped in flag), the author in GoKL cap, Emmett Quigley of MCSF, and forzaminardi.com founder Robert-Jan Bartunek wears the green shirt. (Courtesy Simon Vigar)

"Prior to Alex signing up for the Minardi drive, I tended to support McLaren and my F1 experience was mainly at the Australian and Malaysian GPs. With Minardi, I discovered a team that put extraordinary effort and dedication into making it onto the grid. As an Aussie, I guess I usually like to support the 'underdog' and Minardi certainly was at the underdog end of the ranking and usually the grid. Regardless of which side you're on, if you get involved in a struggle, a sport, or competition, you learn about that endeavour. In fact, supporting Minardi gave opportunities which would be rare with the bigger teams: visits to the garage, talking with Stoddie, drivers, engineers, mechanics and pit crew. Then came the forzaminardi.com site, where we could exchange views, albeit it sometimes anonymously, with other members. I have friends on the board who will always be welcome at my home and in my life. The site is also a great leveller where everyone can have and express his opinion. It is also the place where one can express pride in the efforts and achievements of the team and those who have been there at some time and gone onto greatness, or just loved the sport for the racing."
John Castleman, Kuala Lumpur, Malaysia. [Dr Spin; stepfather of Alex Yoong]

"I think it all started in 1997 when Ukyo Katayama and Tarso Marques were battling it out in the Mild Seven-sponsored and Briatore-owned Minardi-Hart. I was quite amazed that such a small team would fight the odds and still remain unique by designing its own car and keeping its own identity. Throughout the season I saw Minardi fans everywhere and especially the fan club in Montreal caught my attention. In F1, supporters' allegiances seem to be changing like the wind and the bulk of fans change their gear from red to silver and back again every season, depending on who's winning. As a Minardi fan you stayed committed and noticed the great amount of talent they brought into the sport, while coming up with their very own solutions to various problems."
Robert-Jan Bartunek, Innsbruck, Austria [founder of forzaminardi.com]

"I am a Johnny-come-lately Minardi fan. Always an interested spectator of the sport, my interest has waxed and waned over the decades according to whatever else was in my life and occupying my interest at the time. When Paul Stoddart purchased the Minardi team, it seemed that 1980 had come again. There was an Aussie in the sport! My hitherto unfocussed interest in Formula 1 had something to latch on to. That he chose Minardi was a bit odd. Why bother with that particular team? Parked in the back-blocks of Italy with, in all fairness, a laughable history of achievement in the sport. Clearly, the plan was to move the thing to Stoddart's racing base in England and start to build a proper team. But that failed to happen. Like Stoddart, I came to realize that there was a lot to this team. The shy, smiling patriarch who's name the team bears had a citadel of good wishes built around him, by not only countless adoring fans, but by his own employees (including former drivers) as well, and perhaps more importantly still, the Formula 1 establishment. Minardi was Minardi. It was worth something, and like anything that has its value in its history, it was worth keeping. So I became a Minardi fan. One of those people who parade around the general admission areas of the world's Formula 1 venues, shamelessly clothed in Minardi stuff. Normal fans don't understand them. 'How can you be interested in a team that finishes laps behind the field?' they wonder. Keep quiet and try to smile enigmatically is the only way to respond. One of the best things about being a Minardi fan is that it means something different to each person. There are factions that idolize Gian Carlo and despise anything that purports to be Minardi that does not have his imprimatur. Others, like me, like to see the name heading in new directions, and feel that a significant part of what makes the team special is the imprint of the personalities that have contributed to the making of Minardi over the decades. Whatever their views, Minardi fans have shown that they never give up.

"All those years of waiting for the win that never came has taught them patience. So now, even though there is no Minardi Formula 1 team, there are still thousands of active Minardi fans following the fortunes of at least three racing teams that bear the name and waiting, waiting for the next chance at the big game, and I'm there with them."
Wayne Sillick, Canberra, Australia [Lease]

"I believe I found Minardi in 1999 or 2000, loved the livery. It was also when I started to realize what 'The Other Italian Team' was about through their actions in subsequent years. As I have seen personally and heard of from stories on forzaminardi.com and the Minardi Club San Francisco, Minardi actually cared about fans and the racing, not sales of road cars. The team's never-give-up attitude and ability to wring out the most from their equipment and employees with the smallest budget is admirable along with Gian Carlo Minardi's continued development of young talent."
Michael Kilpatrick, Sugar Land, Texas, USA [Telstar]

"I was a Ferrari and Schumacher fan in the late 90s until my eyes noticed a jet black car with a young man named Alonso. Murray Walker used to say they were the smallest team, but every other team envied their closeness and, of course, the best coffee on the grid! I was hooked! A crazy Australian had taken over and the super effort to get to the first race on the grid sealed the deal. Minardi was the team for me. Looking back now, how did I ever follow the unemotional, almost sterile statistical machine that is team Red? Schumacher is still the most skilful driver I have ever seen, but it's heart that counts and Minardi (and its fans) have a big one."
Anastasios Mangos, Canberra, Australia [TasM]

"I first got into F1 by following a guy called Ukyo Katayama. I have no idea why, maybe as I was young and just liked his name. The last team Ukyo drove for was Minardi so after he left F1 I decided just to follow this little team and their drivers. Minardi will always have a place in my heart as they weren't the quickest, nor the richest, but they continued racing for the love of the sport. The little success they had felt like winning the championship."
Kevin McGuire, Aberdeen, Scotland [Minardi4eva]

"I was what, I suppose, would be best described as a casual F1 fan; I'd watch but it was mainly because of the amazement at the speed and handling of these cars. I would hear reference to the Minardi team but that was about it. Then Stoddie turned up and from there I found the forzaminardi website and a group of fans that were more passionate than any Ferrari tifosi could possibly hope to be. I'm still here and have no intention of leaving. Even before Stoddie came along, the 'Minardi' way was more 'Australian' than it probably knew."
Peter Lawson, Melbourne, Australia [oznomad]

"I first started supporting Minardi at the tender age of 13. I remember it like it was yesterday; it was 1995 and my Dad was watching the Grand Prix. I knew little about the sport at that time but as the positions came along the screen this name just hit me, the name was Lamy. I just had to keep watching to see which team he was driving for. Then, for a second, it was there, this nice looking green and white machine. After that I was hooked. But as Pedro Lamy drifted away from F1 there was only thing I wanted to do, support the team that captured my heart."
Mark Shakespeare, Barnsley, UK [Lamy]

"For me, I saw Formula 1 for many years through 'Rosso Corso' eyes. Willing those scarlet (then day-glow red) cars to the top spot on the podium. Only to be left disappointed at season end. Then the Schumacher juggernaut rolled into Maranello. I saw a driver racing as hard as he could against the might of Britain and I was hooked. Then a race in Jerez changed that. Win at all costs is not what sport should be. 'Punching above your weight' is something many Australian sports people are used to. It is something that I found at Minardi. I suddenly got my passion back. I could see this team competing against the corporate might of the pit lane and was never intimidated. Money can sometimes buy success but it cannot buy passion. Minardi exudes passion. Sadly, the Minardi name is missing in F1, but the careers spawned by the team are still there. We just wait for the next world champ. Forza Minardi!"
Joe Capacchione, Melbourne, Australia [SuperRoo]

"I paid Minardi very little attention but then seemingly out of the blue (I would guess that it was 1989) they battled hard and started getting in the points.
At the time I thought 'wouldn't it be funny if the little team could beat the McLarens and Williams?' I thought a little more and decided that it wouldn't just be 'funny' it would be 'great', and that became my dream."
Eddie Dawson-Jones, Holmfirth, UK [JumpeySpyder]

"With no American drivers, there was no logical team or driver for me to like, so I looked to the back of the grid, much the same as I had done in NASCAR. Justin Wilson seemed to make more of a bad car than anyone else, and Verstappen was clearly a wasted talent (and has been my favorite driver since then). I looked around the internet for information about the team, and stumbled upon their official website forum. I found the fans to be as friendly and likable

as the team, and have remained a Minardi fan ever since."
Matt Rekart, Kirkwood, Missouri, USA [Rekart]

"In 2000, Gaston Mazzacane's gallant defence of his position against Mika Hakkinen inspired me to follow the team. Fernando Alonso impressed from the very first race and I was hooked. Minardi moments were rare but always sweet. Mark Webber's points on debut and Zsolt Baumgartner's well deserved eighth place in Indianapolis just days after the birth of my son have cemented the team's place in my heart."
Marc Sparks, Durban, South Africa [Alloy]

"I just knew after my trip to the 1999 Italian GP Minardi were inspirational, and that I had to be involved in supporting them. The return of F1 to the States was in 2000. My friends and I were going to be there and support our guys in person. I flew all night in my work clothes to get there on Thursday in advance of the other members of the club. We had grown to five by now and four of us were going to be there. I saw my first Minardi person at the entrance – a chubby fellow who was dressed in his Telefonica livery – now one of my favourites. I only knew three names from the Minardi organisation – GCM, Roberta and some guy named Massimo. I waved the mechanic down and told him who I was and asked for Massimo. He turned out to be a Brit – one of the few at that time – and he was surprised they had a club in San Francisco. He said he'd send "Mas-I-Mo" out to meet with me. It seemed like forever but this guy eventually came out (looking quite confused) and introduced himself as Massimo Rivola - the then sponsor-handler. I told him who I was and again the reply was 'I did not know we had a club in SF.' I told him we were for real and that I tried to get in touch, yadda yadda, BUT I was unable to contact him. I asked if I could get my people - who were still en route to Indy by plane - to meet with the team. He said that was impossible, but if I wanted to come in then and now he'd get me a pass for one hour. I took the pass and made a fool of myself, I am sure, taking it all in. But no Mr Minardi. Until I left.

Not wanting to wear out my welcome, I returned my pass to Massimo and thanked him profusely before running straight into Gian Carlo Minardi. I almost knocked him down – I then introduced myself and spoke so fast and darn near shook his arm off – he must have thought I was mad. After I calmed down he just took my hand again and said – in English – "Thank you" and went on his way. Since then Minardi, not GCM, nor anybody in particular, just 'Minardi' has been so good to each and every member of the Minardi Club San Francisco as well as fans from all around the globe. All because we support them.
Emmett Quigley, San Francisco, USA. [MCSF]

"My interest in F1 started in 1979 with Gilles Villeneuve. Since then, I have been hooked on F1, big time. In 1985, a small team entered the circus; Minardi. In a period where we saw a lot of teams enter and drop out of F1 (Onyx, Life, Coloni, Andrea Moda, Lambo, Larousse, AGS, etc), Minardi was there, fighting it out in a smart, fair and responsible manner. And they had some of the most beautiful cars on the grid. Then in 1998, my Dad tells me about the existence of an F1 club in Montreal he overheard on the Italian Radio Station, CFMB. When I showed up at the bar, the club in question was the Minardi Club Montreal. A fan club, dedicated to a genuine F1 team. Heading it were a bunch of enthusiasts who saw far and had wild ideas. My first experience was the visit to the Minardi pits the Wednesday before the race. It was great. Then we had a dinner with Esteban Tuero. We were directly connected to the team! Year after year, it only got better. The team was super nice to us, and Mr Minardi a class act. We had a good thing going, making it into the newspapers, Montreal TV, RAI International, Gazzetta dello Sport, and international magazines. Success came easy, because the team made it easy for us. Mr Stoddart then stepped in. Like him or hate him, he too was very good to us and we appreciated that. Then the team was sold to Red Bull and the Minardi name was no more. A cold shower for all us. A lot of the great guys and gals are still at Faenza and we wish them the best of luck!"
Phil Grana, Laval, Quebec, Canada [minardimontreal]

(Courtesy Grand Prix data book)

Key to result codes:

ap	also practiced (in Friday test)	exc	excluded	ns	did not start	ew	entry withdrawn
dq	disqualified	nc	non classified	r	retired	nq	did not qualify

Date	Grand Prix	Circuit	Driver	No	Model	Engine	Config	Notes	Grid	Result
1985										
07/04	BRAZIL	Rio de Janeiro	Pierluigi Martini	29	M185	Ford Cosworth	V8	electrics	25	r
21/04	PORTUGAL	Estoril	Pierluigi Martini	29	M185	Ford Cosworth	V8	spin	25	r
05/05	SAN MARINO	Imola	Pierluigi Martini	29	M185	Motori Moderni	V6t	turbo	19	r
19/05	MONACO	Monte-Carlo	Pierluigi Martini	29	M185	Motori Moderni	V6t	accident/ injury		nq
16/06	CANADA	Montréal	Pierluigi Martini	29	M185	Motori Moderni	V6t	accident	25	r
23/06	USA	Detroit	Pierluigi Martini	29	M185	Motori Moderni	V6t	turbo	25	r
07/07	FRANCE	Paul Ricard	Pierluigi Martini	29	M185	Motori Moderni	V6t	accident	24	r
21/07	BRITAIN	Silverstone	Pierluigi Martini	29	M185	Motori Moderni	V6t	transmission	23	r
04/08	GERMANY	Nürburgring	Pierluigi Martini	29	M185	Motori Moderni	V6t	engine	27	11r
18/08	AUSTRIA	Österreichring	Pierluigi Martini	29	M185	Motori Moderni	V6t	engine	26	r
25/08	NETHERLANDS	Zandvoort	Pierluigi Martini	29	M185	Motori Moderni	V6t	accident	24	r
08/09	ITALY	Monza	Pierluigi Martini	29	M185	Motori Moderni	V6t	fuel pump	23	r
15/09	BELGIUM	Spa-Francorchamps	Pierluigi Martini	29	M185	Motori Moderni	V6t		24	12
06/10	EUROPE	Brands Hatch	Pierluigi Martini	29	M185	Motori Moderni	V6t	accident	26	r
19/10	SOUTH AFRICA	Kyalami	Pierluigi Martini	29	M185	Motori Moderni	V6t	radiator	19	r
03/11	AUSTRALIA	Adelaide	Pierluigi Martini	29	M185	Motori Moderni	V6t		23	8
1986										
23/03	BRAZIL	Rio de Janeiro	Andrea de Cesaris	23	M185B	Motori Moderni	V6t	turbo	22	r
			Alessandro Nannini	24	M185B	Motori Moderni	V6t	clutch	25	r
13/04	SPAIN	Jerez de la Frontera	Andrea de Cesaris	23	M185B	Motori Moderni	V6t	differential	24	r

			Alessandro Nannini	24	M185B	Motori Moderni	V6t	differential on parade lap	25	ns
27/04	SAN MARINO	Imola	Andrea de Cesaris	23	M185B	Motori Moderni	V6t	engine	23	r
			Alessandro Nannini	24	M185B	Motori Moderni	V6t	accident	18	r
11/05	MONACO	Monte-Carlo	Andrea de Cesaris	23	M185B	Motori Moderni	V6t			nq
			Alessandro Nannini	24	M185B	Motori Moderni	V6t			nq
25/05	BELGIUM	Spa-Francorchamps	Andrea de Cesaris	23	M185B	Motori Moderni	V6t	out of fuel	19	r
			Alessandro Nannini	24	M185B	Motori Moderni	V6t	gearbox	22	r
15/06	CANADA	Montréal	Andrea de Cesaris	23	M185B	Motori Moderni	V6t	gearbox	20	r
			Alessandro Nannini	24	M185B	Motori Moderni	V6t	turbo	19	r
22/06	USA	Detroit	Andrea de Cesaris	23	M185B	Motori Moderni	V6t	gearbox	23	r
			Alessandro Nannini	24	M185B	Motori Moderni	V6t	turbo	24	r
06/07	FRANCE	Paul Ricard	Andrea de Cesaris	23	M185B	Motori Moderni	V6t	turbo	23	r
			Alessandro Nannini	24	M185B	Motori Moderni	V6t	accident	19	r
13/07	BRITAIN	Brands Hatch	Andrea de Cesaris	23	M185B	Motori Moderni	V6t	alternator	21	r
			Alessandro Nannini	24	M185B	Motori Moderni	V6t	cv joint	20	r
27/07	GERMANY	Hockenheim	Andrea de Cesaris	23	M185B	Motori Moderni	V6t	gearbox	23	r
			Alessandro Nannini	24	M185B	Motori Moderni	V6t	engine overheating	22	r
10/08	HUNGARY	Hungaroring	Andrea de Cesaris	23	M186	Motori Moderni	V6t	engine	20	r
			Alessandro Nannini	24	M185B	Motori Moderni	V6t	engine	17	r
17/08	AUSTRIA	Österreichring	Andrea de Cesaris	23	M186	Motori Moderni	V6t	driveshaft	23	r
			Alessandro Nannini	24	M185B	Motori Moderni	V6t	rear suspension/ spin	19	r
07/09	ITALY	Monza	Andrea de Cesaris	23	M186	Motori Moderni	V6t	engine	21	r
			Alessandro Nannini	24	M185B	Motori Moderni	V6t	alternator belt	19	r
21/09	PORTUGAL	Estoril	Andrea de Cesaris	23	M186	Motori Moderni	V6t	accident	16	r
			Alessandro Nannini	24	M185B	Motori Moderni	V6t	gearbox	18	r
12/10	MEXICO	Mexico City	Andrea de Cesaris	23	M186	Motori Moderni	V6t		22	8
			Alessandro Nannini	24	M185B	Motori Moderni	V6t		24	14
26/10	AUSTRALIA	Adelaide	Andrea de Cesaris	23	M186	Motori Moderni	V6t	fire extinguisher	11	r
			Alessandro Nannini	24	M185B	Motori Moderni	V6t	accident	18	r
1987										
12/04	BRAZIL	Rio de Janeiro	Adrian Campos	23	M187	Motori Moderni	V6t	overtook on parade lap	16	dq
			Alessandro Nannini	24	M187	Motori Moderni	V6t	suspension/ accident	15	r
03/05	SAN MARINO	Imola	Adrian Campos	23	M187	Motori Moderni	V6t	gearbox	16	r
			Alessandro Nannini	24	M187	Motori Moderni	V6t	engine	15	r
17/05	BELGIUM	Spa-Francorchamps	Adrian Campos	23	M187	Motori Moderni	V6t	oil pressure	19	r
			Alessandro Nannini	24	M187	Motori Moderni	V6t	turbo	14	r
31/05	MONACO	Monte-Carlo	Adrian Campos	23	M187	Motori Moderni	V6t	accident/ injury		ns
			Alessandro Nannini	24	M187	Motori Moderni	V6t	electrics	13	r
21/06	USA	Detroit	Adrian Campos	23	M187	Motori Moderni	V6t	accident	25	r
			Alessandro Nannini	24	M187	Motori Moderni	V6t	gearbox	18	r
05/07	FRANCE	Paul Ricard	Adrian Campos	23	M187	Motori Moderni	V6t	turbo	21	r

			Alessandro Nannini	24	M187	Motori Moderni	V6t	turbo	15	r
12/07	BRITAIN	Silverstone	Adrian Campos	23	M187	Motori Moderni	V6t	fuel pump	19	r
			Alessandro Nannini	24	M187	Motori Moderni	V6t	engine	15	r
26/07	GERMANY	Hockenheim	Adrian Campos	23	M187	Motori Moderni	V6t	engine	18	r
			Alessandro Nannini	24	M187	Motori Moderni	V6t	engine	16	r
09/08	HUNGARY	Hungaroring	Adrian Campos	23	M187	Motori Moderni	V6t	accident	24	r
			Alessandro Nannini	24	M187	Motori Moderni	V6t		20	11
16/08	AUSTRIA	Österreichring	Adrian Campos	23	M187	Motori Moderni	V6t	distributor belt	19	r
			Alessandro Nannini	24	M187	Motori Moderni	V6t	engine	15	r
06/09	ITALY	Monza	Adrian Campos	23	M187	Motori Moderni	V6t	fuel filter/ fire	20	r
			Alessandro Nannini	24	M187	Motori Moderni	V6t	out of fuel	18	16r
20/09	PORTUGAL	Estoril	Adrian Campos	23	M187	Motori Moderni	V6t	intercooler	20	r
			Alessandro Nannini	24	M187	Motori Moderni	V6t	out of fuel	14	11r
27/09	SPAIN	Jerez de la Frontera	Adrian Campos	23	M187	Motori Moderni	V6t		24	14
			Alessandro Nannini	24	M187	Motori Moderni	V6t	turbo	21	r
18/10	MEXICO	Mexico City	Adrian Campos	23	M187	Motori Moderni	V6t	gear linkage	19	r
			Alessandro Nannini	24	M187	Motori Moderni	V6t	turbo	14	r
01/11	JAPAN	Suzuka	Adrian Campos	23	M187	Motori Moderni	V6t	engine	21	r
			Alessandro Nannini	24	M187	Motori Moderni	V6t	engine	14	r
15/11	AUSTRALIA	Adelaide	Adrian Campos	23	M187	Motori Moderni	V6t	gearbox	26	r
			Alessandro Nannini	24	M187	Motori Moderni	V6t	accident	13	r
1988										
03/04	BRAZIL	Rio de Janeiro	Adrian Campos	23	M188	Ford Cosworth	V8	rear wing mounting	23	r
			Luis Sala	24	M188	Ford Cosworth	V8	rear wing mounting	20	r
01/05	SAN MARINO	Imola	Adrian Campos	23	M188	Ford Cosworth	V8		22	16
			Luis Sala	24	M188	Ford Cosworth	V8		18	11
15/05	MONACO	Monte-Carlo	Adrian Campos	23	M188	Ford Cosworth	V8			nq
			Luis Sala	24	M188	Ford Cosworth	V8	driveshafts	15	r
29/05	MEXICO	Mexico City	Adrian Campos	23	M188	Ford Cosworth	V8			nq
			Luis Sala	24	M188	Ford Cosworth	V8		25	11
12/06	CANADA	Montréal	Adrian Campos	23	M188	Ford Cosworth	V8			nq
			Luis Sala	24	M188	Ford Cosworth	V8		21	13
19/06	USA	Detroit	Pierluigi Martini	23	M188	Ford Cosworth	V8		16	6
			Luis Sala	24	M188	Ford Cosworth	V8	gearbox	25	r
03/07	FRANCE	Paul Ricard	Pierluigi Martini	23	M188	Ford Cosworth	V8		22	15
			Luis Sala	24	M188	Ford Cosworth	V8		25	nc
10/07	BRITAIN	Silverstone	Pierluigi Martini	23	M188	Ford Cosworth	V8		19	15
			Luis Sala	24	M188	Ford Cosworth	V8	accident	18	r
24/07	GERMANY	Hockenheim	Pierluigi Martini	23	M188	Ford Cosworth	V8			nq
			Luis Sala	24	M188	Ford Cosworth	V8			nq
07/08	HUNGARY	Hungaroring	Pierluigi Martini	23	M188	Ford Cosworth	V8	accident	16	r

			Luis Sala	24	M188	Ford Cosworth	V8		11	10
28/08	BELGIUM	Spa-Francorchamps	Pierluigi Martini	23	M188	Ford Cosworth	V8			nq
			Luis Sala	24	M188	Ford Cosworth	V8			nq
11/09	ITALY	Monza	Pierluigi Martini	23	M188	Ford Cosworth	V8	engine	14	r
			Luis Sala	24	M188	Ford Cosworth	V8	gearbox	19	r
25/09	PORTUGAL	Estoril	Pierluigi Martini	23	M188	Ford Cosworth	V8	engine	14	r
			Luis Sala	24	M188	Ford Cosworth	V8		19	8
02/10	SPAIN	Jerez de la Frontera	Pierluigi Martini	23	M188	Ford Cosworth	V8	gearbox	20	r
			Luis Sala	24	M188	Ford Cosworth	V8		24	12
30/10	JAPAN	Suzuka	Pierluigi Martini	23	M188	Ford Cosworth	V8		17	13
			Luis Sala	24	M188	Ford Cosworth	V8		22	15
13/11	AUSTRALIA	Adelaide	Pierluigi Martini	23	M188	Ford Cosworth	V8		14	7
			Luis Sala	24	M188	Ford Cosworth	V8	engine	21	r
1989										
26/03	BRAZIL	Rio de Janeiro	Pierluigi Martini	23	M188B	Ford Cosworth	V8	engine mounting	16	r
			Luis Sala	24	M188B	Ford Cosworth	V8	accident	23	r
23/04	SAN MARINO	Imola	Pierluigi Martini	23	M188B	Ford Cosworth	V8	gearbox	11	r
			Luis Sala	24	M188B	Ford Cosworth	V8	accident	15	r
07/05	MONACO	Monte-Carlo	Pierluigi Martini	23	M188B	Ford Cosworth	V8	clutch	11	r
			Luis Sala	24	M188B	Ford Cosworth	V8	engine/ fire	26	r
28/05	MEXICO	Mexico City	Pierluigi Martini	23	M189	Ford Cosworth	V8	engine	22	r
			Luis Sala	24	M189	Ford Cosworth	V8			nq
04/06	USA	Phoenix	Pierluigi Martini	23	M189	Ford Cosworth	V8	engine overheating	15	r
			Luis Sala	24	M189	Ford Cosworth	V8	engine overheating	20	r
18/06	CANADA	Montréal	Pierluigi Martini	23	M189	Ford Cosworth	V8	accident	11	r
			Luis Sala	24	M189	Ford Cosworth	V8	accident	24	r
09/07	FRANCE	Paul Ricard	Pierluigi Martini	23	M189	Ford Cosworth	V8	oil pressure	23	r
			Luis Sala	24	M189	Ford Cosworth	V8			nq
16/07	BRITAIN	Silverstone	Pierluigi Martini	23	M189	Ford Cosworth	V8		11	5
			Luis Sala	24	M189	Ford Cosworth	V8		15	6
30/07	GERMANY	Hockenheim	Pierluigi Martini	23	M189	Ford Cosworth	V8		13	9
			Luis Sala	24	M189	Ford Cosworth	V8			nq
13/08	HUNGARY	Hungaroring	Pierluigi Martini	23	M189	Ford Cosworth	V8	wheel bearings/ brake fire	10	r
			Luis Sala	24	M189	Ford Cosworth	V8	accident	23	r
27/08	BELGIUM	Spa-Francorchamps	Pierluigi Martini	23	M189	Ford Cosworth	V8		14	9
			Luis Sala	24	M189	Ford Cosworth	V8		25	15
10/09	ITALY	Monza	Pierluigi Martini	23	M189	Ford Cosworth	V8		15	7
			Luis Sala	24	M189	Ford Cosworth	V8		26	8
24/09	PORTUGAL	Estoril	Pierluigi Martini	23	M189	Ford Cosworth	V8		5	5
			Luis Sala	24	M189	Ford Cosworth	V8		9	12
01/10	SPAIN	Jerez de la Frontera	Pierluigi Martini	23	M189	Ford Cosworth	V8	spin	4	r

			Luis Sala	24	M189	Ford Cosworth	V8	accident	20	r
22/10	JAPAN	Suzuka	Paolo Barilla	23	M189	Ford Cosworth	V8	clutch	19	r
			Luis Sala	24	M189	Ford Cosworth	V8	accident	14	r
05/11	AUSTRALIA	Adelaide	Pierluigi Martini	23	M189	Ford Cosworth	V8		3	6
			Luis Sala	24	M189	Ford Cosworth	V8			nq
1990										
11/03	USA	Phoenix	Pierluigi Martini	23	M189	Ford Cosworth	V8		2	7
			Paolo Barilla	24	M189	Ford Cosworth	V8	driver discomfort (arm cramp)	14	r
25/03	BRAZIL	Interlagos	Pierluigi Martini	23	M189	Ford Cosworth	V8		8	9
			Paolo Barilla	24	M189	Ford Cosworth	V8	engine	17	r
13/05	SAN MARINO	Imola	Pierluigi Martini	23	M190	Ford Cosworth	V8	accident/ injury		ns
			Paolo Barilla	24	M190	Ford Cosworth	V8		26	11
27/05	MONACO	Monte-Carlo	Pierluigi Martini	23	M190	Ford Cosworth	V8	ignition	8	r
			Paolo Barilla	24	M190	Ford Cosworth	V8	gearbox	19	r
10/06	CANADA	Montréal	Pierluigi Martini	23	M190	Ford Cosworth	V8	spin	16	r
			Paolo Barilla	24	M190	Ford Cosworth	V8			nq
24/06	MEXICO	Mexico City	Pierluigi Martini	23	M190	Ford Cosworth	V8		7	12
			Paolo Barilla	24	M190	Ford Cosworth	V8		16	14
08/07	FRANCE	Paul Ricard	Pierluigi Martini	23	M190	Ford Cosworth	V8	electrics	23	r
			Paolo Barilla	24	M190	Ford Cosworth	V8			nq
15/07	BRITAIN	Silverstone	Pierluigi Martini	23	M190	Ford Cosworth	V8	alternator	18	r
			Paolo Barilla	24	M190	Ford Cosworth	V8		24	12
29/07	GERMANY	Hockenheim	Pierluigi Martini	23	M190	Ford Cosworth	V8	engine	15	r
			Paolo Barilla	24	M190	Ford Cosworth	V8			nq
12/08	HUNGARY	Hungaroring	Pierluigi Martini	23	M190	Ford Cosworth	V8	accident	14	r
			Paolo Barilla	24	M190	Ford Cosworth	V8		23	15
26/08	BELGIUM	Spa-Francorchamps	Pierluigi Martini	23	M190	Ford Cosworth	V8		16	15
			Paolo Barilla	24	M190	Ford Cosworth	V8	accident *	25	r
09/09	ITALY	Monza	Pierluigi Martini	23	M190	Ford Cosworth	V8	spin/ rear suspension	15	r
			Paolo Barilla	24	M190	Ford Cosworth	V8			nq
23/09	PORTUGAL	Estoril	Pierluigi Martini	23	M190	Ford Cosworth	V8		16	11
			Paolo Barilla	24	M190	Ford Cosworth	V8			nq
30/09	SPAIN	Jerez de la Frontera	Pierluigi Martini	23	M190	Ford Cosworth	V8	wheel nut loose/ spin	11	r
			Paolo Barilla	24	M190	Ford Cosworth	V8			nq
21/10	JAPAN	Suzuka	Pierluigi Martini	23	M190	Ford Cosworth	V8		10	8
			Gianni Morbidelli	24	M190	Ford Cosworth	V8	spin	19	r
04/11	AUSTRALIA	Adelaide	Pierluigi Martini	23	M190	Ford Cosworth	V8		10	9
			Gianni Morbidelli	24	M190	Ford Cosworth	V8	gearbox	20	r

* = retired after second start

1991										
10/03	USA	Phoenix	Pierluigi Martini	23	M191	Ferrari	V12	engine	15	9r
			Gianni Morbidelli	24	M191	Ferrari	V12	gearbox	26	r
24/03	BRAZIL	Interlagos	Pierluigi Martini	23	M191	Ferrari	V12	spin	20	r
			Gianni Morbidelli	24	M191	Ferrari	V12		21	8
28/04	SAN MARINO	Imola	Pierluigi Martini	23	M191	Ferrari	V12		9	4
			Gianni Morbidelli	24	M191	Ferrari	V12	gearbox	8	r
12/05	MONACO	Monte-Carlo	Pierluigi Martini	23	M191	Ferrari	V12		14	12
			Gianni Morbidelli	24	M191	Ferrari	V12	gearbox	17	r
02/06	CANADA	Montréal	Pierluigi Martini	23	M191	Ferrari	V12		18	7
			Gianni Morbidelli	24	M191	Ferrari	V12	spin	15	r
16/06	MEXICO	Mexico City	Pierluigi Martini	23	M191	Ferrari	V12	spin	15	r
			Gianni Morbidelli	24	M191	Ferrari	V12		23	7
07/07	FRANCE	Magny-Cours	Pierluigi Martini	23	M191	Ferrari	V12		12	9
			Gianni Morbidelli	24	M191	Ferrari	V12	accident	10	r
14/07	BRITAIN	Silverstone	Pierluigi Martini	23	M191	Ferrari	V12		23	9
			Gianni Morbidelli	24	M191	Ferrari	V12		20	11
28/07	GERMANY	Hockenheim	Pierluigi Martini	23	M191	Ferrari	V12	engine/ spin	10	r
			Gianni Morbidelli	24	M191	Ferrari	V12	engine	19	r
11/08	HUNGARY	Hungaroring	Pierluigi Martini	23	M191	Ferrari	V12	engine	18	r
			Gianni Morbidelli	24	M191	Ferrari	V12		23	13
25/08	BELGIUM	Spa-Francorchamps	Pierluigi Martini	23	M191	Ferrari	V12		9	12
			Gianni Morbidelli	24	M191	Ferrari	V12	engine	19	r
08/09	ITALY	Monza	Pierluigi Martini	23	M191	Ferrari	V12	brakes/ spin	10	r
			Gianni Morbidelli	24	M191	Ferrari	V12		17	9
22/09	PORTUGAL	Estoril	Pierluigi Martini	23	M191	Ferrari	V12		8	4
			Gianni Morbidelli	24	M191	Ferrari	V12		13	9
29/09	SPAIN	Montmeló	Pierluigi Martini	23	M191	Ferrari	V12		19	13
			Gianni Morbidelli	24	M191	Ferrari	V12	accident	16	14r
20/10	JAPAN	Suzuka	Pierluigi Martini	23	M191	Ferrari	V12	clutch	7	r
			Gianni Morbidelli	24	M191	Ferrari	V12	wheel bearing	8	r
03/11	AUSTRALIA	Adelaide	Pierluigi Martini	23	M191	Ferrari	V12	accident	10	r
			Roberto Moreno	24	M191	Ferrari	V12		18	16
1992										
01/03	SOUTH AFRICA	Kyalami	Christian Fittipaldi	23	M191B	Lamborghini	V12	electrics	20	r
			Gianni Morbidelli	24	M191B	Lamborghini	V12	engine	19	r
22/03	MEXICO	Mexico City	Christian Fittipaldi	23	M191B	Lamborghini	V12	spin	17	r
			Gianni Morbidelli	24	M191B	Lamborghini	V12	spin	21	r
05/04	BRAZIL	Interlagos	Christian Fittipaldi	23	M191B	Lamborghini	V12	gearbox	20	r
			Gianni Morbidelli	24	M191B	Lamborghini	V12		23	7
03/05	SPAIN	Montmeló	Christian Fittipaldi	23	M191B	Lamborghini	V12		22	11

			Gianni Morbidelli	24	M191B	Lamborghini	V12	handling	25	r
17/05	SAN MARINO	Imola	Christian Fittipaldi	23	M192	Lamborghini	V12	transmission	25	r
			Gianni Morbidelli	24	M192	Lamborghini	V12	transmission	21	r
31/05	MONACO	Monte-Carlo	Christian Fittipaldi	23	M192	Lamborghini	V12		17	8
			Gianni Morbidelli	24	M192	Lamborghini	V12	battery	12	r
14/06	CANADA	Montréal	Christian Fittipaldi	23	M192	Lamborghini	V12	gearbox oil fire	25	13r
			Gianni Morbidelli	24	M192	Lamborghini	V12		13	11
05/07	FRANCE	Magny-Cours	Christian Fittipaldi	23	M192	Lamborghini	V12	accident/ injury		nq
			Gianni Morbidelli	24	M192	Lamborghini	V12		16	8
12/07	BRITAIN	Silverstone	Alessandro Zanardi	23	M192	Lamborghini	V12			nq
			Gianni Morbidelli	24	M192	Lamborghini	V12	oil pressure	25	17r
26/07	GERMANY	Hockenheim	Alessandro Zanardi	23	M192	Lamborghini	V12	clutch	24	r
			Gianni Morbidelli	24	M192	Lamborghini	V12		26	12
16/08	HUNGARY	Hungaroring	Alessandro Zanardi	23	M192	Lamborghini	V12			nq
			Gianni Morbidelli	24	M192	Lamborghini	V12			nq
30/08	BELGIUM	Spa-Francorchamps	Christian Fittipaldi	23	M192	Lamborghini	V12			nq
			Gianni Morbidelli	24	M192	Lamborghini	V12		23	16
13/09	ITALY	Monza	Christian Fittipaldi	23	M192	Lamborghini	V12			nq
			Gianni Morbidelli	24	M192	Lamborghini	V12	engine	12	r
27/09	PORTUGAL	Estoril	Christian Fittipaldi	23	M192	Lamborghini	V12		26	12
			Gianni Morbidelli	24	M192	Lamborghini	V12		18	14
25/10	JAPAN	Suzuka	Christian Fittipaldi	23	M192	Lamborghini	V12		12	6
			Gianni Morbidelli	24	M192	Lamborghini	V12		14	14
08/11	AUSTRALIA	Adelaide	Christian Fittipaldi	23	M192	Lamborghini	V12		17	9
			Gianni Morbidelli	24	M192	Lamborghini	V12		16	10
1993										
14/03	SOUTH AFRICA	Kyalami	Christian Fittipaldi	23	M193	Ford Cosworth	V8		13	4
			Fabrizio Barbazza	24	M193	Ford Cosworth	V8	accident	24	r
28/03	BRAZIL	Interlagos	Christian Fittipaldi	23	M193	Ford Cosworth	V8	accident	20	r
			Fabrizio Barbazza	24	M193	Ford Cosworth	V8	accident	24	r
11/04	EUROPE	Donington Park	Christian Fittipaldi	23	M193	Ford Cosworth	V8		16	7
			Fabrizio Barbazza	24	M193	Ford Cosworth	V8		20	6
25/04	SAN MARINO	Imola	Christian Fittipaldi	23	M193	Ford Cosworth	V8	steering	23	r
			Fabrizio Barbazza	24	M193	Ford Cosworth	V8		25	6
09/05	SPAIN	Montmeló	Christian Fittipaldi	23	M193	Ford Cosworth	V8		20	8
			Fabrizio Barbazza	24	M193	Ford Cosworth	V8	accident	25	r
23/05	MONACO	Monte-Carlo	Christian Fittipaldi	23	M193	Ford Cosworth	V8		17	5
			Fabrizio Barbazza	24	M193	Ford Cosworth	V8		25	11
13/06	CANADA	Montréal	Christian Fittipaldi	23	M193	Ford Cosworth	V8		17	9
			Fabrizio Barbazza	24	M193	Ford Cosworth	V8	gearbox	23	r
04/07	FRANCE	Magny-Cours	Christian Fittipaldi	23	M193	Ford Cosworth	V8		23	8

			Fabrizio Barbazza	24	M193	Ford Cosworth	V8	gearbox	24	r
11/07	BRITAIN	Silverstone	Christian Fittipaldi	23	M193	Ford Cosworth	V8	gearbox	19	12r
			Pierluigi Martini	24	M193	Ford Cosworth	V8	driver discomfort	20	r
25/07	GERMANY	Hockenheim	Christian Fittipaldi	23	M193	Ford Cosworth	V8		20	11
			Pierluigi Martini	24	M193	Ford Cosworth	V8		22	14
15/08	HUNGARY	Hungaroring	Christian Fittipaldi	23	M193	Ford Cosworth	V8	accident	14	r
			Pierluigi Martini	24	M193	Ford Cosworth	V8	accident	7	r
29/08	BELGIUM	Spa-Francorchamps	Christian Fittipaldi	23	M193	Ford Cosworth	V8	accident	22	r
			Pierluigi Martini	24	M193	Ford Cosworth	V8	spin	21	r
12/09	ITALY	Monza	Christian Fittipaldi	23	M193	Ford Cosworth	V8		24	8
			Pierluigi Martini	24	M193	Ford Cosworth	V8		22	7
26/09	PORTUGAL	Estoril	Christian Fittipaldi	23	M193	Ford Cosworth	V8		24	9
			Pierluigi Martini	24	M193	Ford Cosworth	V8		19	8
24/10	JAPAN	Suzuka	Jean-Marc Gounon	23	M193	Ford Cosworth	V8	engine	24	r
			Pierluigi Martini	24	M193	Ford Cosworth	V8		22	10
07/11	AUSTRALIA	Adelaide	Jean-Marc Gounon	23	M193	Ford Cosworth	V8	spin	22	r
			Pierluigi Martini	24	M193	Ford Cosworth	V8	gearbox	16	r
1994										
27/03	BRAZIL	Interlagos	Pierluigi Martini	23	M193B	Ford Cosworth	V8		15	8
			Michele Alboreto	24	M193B	Ford Cosworth	V8	electrics	22	r
17/04	PACIFIC	Aida	Pierluigi Martini	23	M193B	Ford Cosworth	V8	electrics	17	r
			Michele Alboreto	24	M193B	Ford Cosworth	V8	accident	15	r
01/05	SAN MARINO	Imola	Pierluigi Martini	23	M193B	Ford Cosworth	V8	spin	14	r
			Michele Alboreto	24	M193B	Ford Cosworth	V8	rear wheel lost	15	r
15/05	MONACO	Monte-Carlo	Pierluigi Martini	23	M193B	Ford Cosworth	V8	accident	9	r
			Michele Alboreto	24	M193B	Ford Cosworth	V8		12	6
29/05	SPAIN	Montmeló	Pierluigi Martini	23	M193B	Ford Cosworth	V8		18	5
			Michele Alboreto	24	M193B	Ford Cosworth	V8	engine	14	r
12/06	CANADA	Montréal	Pierluigi Martini	23	M194	Ford Cosworth	V8		15	9
			Michele Alboreto	24	M194	Ford Cosworth	V8		18	11
03/07	FRANCE	Magny-Cours	Pierluigi Martini	23	M194	Ford Cosworth	V8		16	5
			Michele Alboreto	24	M194	Ford Cosworth	V8	engine	21	r
10/07	BRITAIN	Silverstone	Pierluigi Martini	23	M194	Ford Cosworth	V8		14	10
			Michele Alboreto	24	M194	Ford Cosworth	V8	engine	17	r
31/07	GERMANY	Hockenheim	Pierluigi Martini	23	M194	Ford Cosworth	V8	accident	20	r
			Michele Alboreto	24	M194	Ford Cosworth	V8	accident	23	r
14/08	HUNGARY	Hungaroring	Pierluigi Martini	23	M194	Ford Cosworth	V8	spin	15	r
			Michele Alboreto	24	M194	Ford Cosworth	V8		20	7
28/08	BELGIUM	Spa-Francorchamps	Pierluigi Martini	23	M194	Ford Cosworth	V8		10	8
			Michele Alboreto	24	M194	Ford Cosworth	V8		18	9
11/09	ITALY	Monza	Pierluigi Martini	23	M194	Ford Cosworth	V8	spin	18	r

			Michele Alboreto	24	M194	Ford Cosworth	V8	gearbox	22	r
25/09	PORTUGAL	Estoril	Pierluigi Martini	23	M194	Ford Cosworth	V8		18	12
			Michele Alboreto	24	M194	Ford Cosworth	V8		19	13
16/10	EUROPE	Jerez de la Frontera	Pierluigi Martini	23	M194	Ford Cosworth	V8		17	15
			Michele Alboreto	24	M194	Ford Cosworth	V8		20	14
06/11	JAPAN	Suzuka	Pierluigi Martini	23	M194	Ford Cosworth	V8	accident	16	r
			Michele Alboreto	24	M194	Ford Cosworth	V8	spin	21	r
13/11	AUSTRALIA	Adelaide	Pierluigi Martini	23	M194	Ford Cosworth	V8		18	9
			Michele Alboreto	24	M194	Ford Cosworth	V8	accident/ rear suspension	16	r
1995										
26/03	BRAZIL	Interlagos	Pierluigi Martini	23	M195	Ford Cosworth	V8	gearbox on parade lap	17	ns
			Luca Badoer	24	M195	Ford Cosworth	V8	gearbox	18	r
09/04	ARGENTINA	Buenos Aires	Pierluigi Martini	23	M195	Ford Cosworth	V8	spin	16	r
			Luca Badoer	24	M195	Ford Cosworth	V8	accident *	13	r
30/04	SAN MARINO	Imola	Pierluigi Martini	23	M195	Ford Cosworth	V8		18	12
			Luca Badoer	24	M195	Ford Cosworth	V8		20	14
14/05	SPAIN	Montmeló	Pierluigi Martini	23	M195	Ford Cosworth	V8		19	14
			Luca Badoer	24	M195	Ford Cosworth	V8	hydraulics	21	r
28/05	MONACO	Monte-Carlo	Pierluigi Martini	23	M195	Ford Cosworth	V8		18	7
			Luca Badoer	24	M195	Ford Cosworth	V8	accident/ driveshaft/ suspension	16	r
11/06	CANADA	Montréal	Pierluigi Martini	23	M195	Ford Cosworth	V8	throttle linkage	17	r
			Luca Badoer	24	M195	Ford Cosworth	V8		19	8
02/07	FRANCE	Magny-Cours	Pierluigi Martini	23	M195	Ford Cosworth	V8	gearbox	20	r
			Luca Badoer	24	M195	Ford Cosworth	V8		17	13
16/07	BRITAIN	Silverstone	Pierluigi Martini	23	M195	Ford Cosworth	V8		15	7
			Luca Badoer	24	M195	Ford Cosworth	V8		18	10
30/07	GERMANY	Hockenheim	Pierluigi Martini	23	M195	Ford Cosworth	V8	engine	20	r
			Luca Badoer	24	M195	Ford Cosworth	V8	gearbox actuator oil leak	16	r
13/08	HUNGARY	Hungaroring	Pedro Lamy	23	M195	Ford Cosworth	V8		15	9
			Luca Badoer	24	M195	Ford Cosworth	V8		12	8
27/08	BELGIUM	Spa-Francorchamps	Pedro Lamy	23	M195	Ford Cosworth	V8		17	10
			Luca Badoer	24	M195	Ford Cosworth	V8	accident	19	r
10/09	ITALY	Monza	Pedro Lamy	23	M195	Ford Cosworth	V8	differential	19	r
			Luca Badoer	24	M195	Ford Cosworth	V8	accident	18	r
24/09	PORTUGAL	Estoril	Pedro Lamy	23	M195	Ford Cosworth	V8	hydraulics	17	r
			Luca Badoer	24	M195	Ford Cosworth	V8		18	14
01/10	EUROPE	Nürburgring	Pedro Lamy	23	M195	Ford Cosworth	V8		16	9
			Luca Badoer	24	M195	Ford Cosworth	V8		18	11
22/10	PACIFIC	Aida	Pedro Lamy	23	M195	Ford Cosworth	V8		14	13
			Luca Badoer	24	M195	Ford Cosworth	V8		16	15

29/10	JAPAN	Suzuka	Pedro Lamy	23	M195	Ford Cosworth	V8		16	11
			Luca Badoer	24	M195	Ford Cosworth	V8		17	9
12/11	AUSTRALIA	Adelaide	Pedro Lamy	23	M195	Ford Cosworth	V8		17	6
			Luca Badoer	24	M195	Ford Cosworth	V8	electrics on dummy grid	15	ns
										* = retired after first start
1996										
10/03	AUSTRALIA	Melbourne	Pedro Lamy	20	M195B	Ford Cosworth	V8	accident/ loose seat belts	17	r
			Giancarlo Fisichella	21	M195B	Ford Cosworth	V8	clutch	16	r
31/03	BRAZIL	Interlagos	Pedro Lamy	20	M195B	Ford Cosworth	V8		18	10
			Tarso Marques	21	M195B	Ford Cosworth	V8	spin	21	r
07/04	ARGENTINA	Buenos Aires	Pedro Lamy	20	M195B	Ford Cosworth	V8	differential	19	r
			Tarso Marques	21	M195B	Ford Cosworth	V8	accident	14	r
28/04	EUROPE	Nürburgring	Pedro Lamy	20	M195B	Ford Cosworth	V8		19	12
			Giancarlo Fisichella	21	M195B	Ford Cosworth	V8		18	13
05/05	SAN MARINO	Imola	Pedro Lamy	20	M195B	Ford Cosworth	V8		18	9
			Giancarlo Fisichella	21	M195B	Ford Cosworth	V8	engine	19	r
19/05	MONACO	Monte-Carlo	Pedro Lamy	20	M195B	Ford Cosworth	V8	accident	19	r
			Giancarlo Fisichella	21	M195B	Ford Cosworth	V8	accident	18	r
02/06	SPAIN	Montmeló	Pedro Lamy	20	M195B	Ford Cosworth	V8	accident	18	r
			Giancarlo Fisichella	21	M195B	Ford Cosworth	V8	accident damage	19	r
16/06	CANADA	Montréal	Pedro Lamy	20	M195B	Ford Cosworth	V8	accident	19	r
			Giancarlo Fisichella	21	M195B	Ford Cosworth	V8		16	8
30/06	FRANCE	Magny-Cours	Pedro Lamy	20	M195B	Ford Cosworth	V8		18	12
			Giancarlo Fisichella	21	M195B	Ford Cosworth	V8	fuel pump	17	r
14/07	BRITAIN	Silverstone	Pedro Lamy	20	M195B	Ford Cosworth	V8	hydraulics	19	r
			Giancarlo Fisichella	21	M195B	Ford Cosworth	V8		18	11
28/07	GERMANY	Hockenheim	Pedro Lamy	20	M195B	Ford Cosworth	V8		18	12
			Giovanni Lavaggi	21	M195B	Ford Cosworth	V8			nq
11/08	HUNGARY	Hungaroring	Pedro Lamy	20	M195B	Ford Cosworth	V8	accident/ rear suspension	19	r
			Giovanni Lavaggi	21	M195B	Ford Cosworth	V8	spin	20	10r
25/08	BELGIUM	Spa-Francorchamps	Pedro Lamy	20	M195B	Ford Cosworth	V8		19	10
			Giovanni Lavaggi	21	M195B	Ford Cosworth	V8			nq
08/09	ITALY	Monza	Pedro Lamy	20	M195B	Ford Cosworth	V8	engine	18	r
			Giovanni Lavaggi	21	M195B	Ford Cosworth	V8	engine	20	r
22/09	PORTUGAL	Estoril	Pedro Lamy	20	M195B	Ford Cosworth	V8		19	16
			Giovanni Lavaggi	21	M195B	Ford Cosworth	V8		20	15
13/10	JAPAN	Suzuka	Pedro Lamy	20	M195B	Ford Cosworth	V8		18	12
			Giovanni Lavaggi	21	M195B	Ford Cosworth	V8			nq
1997										
09/03	AUSTRALIA	Melbourne	Ukyo Katayama	20	M197	Hart	V8	fuel pump	15	r
			Jarno Trulli	21	M197	Hart	V8		17	9

30/03	BRAZIL	Interlagos	Ukyo Katayama	20	M197	Hart	V8		18	18
			Jarno Trulli	21	M197	Hart	V8		17	12
13/04	ARGENTINA	Buenos Aires	Ukyo Katayama	20	M197	Hart	V8	throttle stuck/ spin	21	r
			Jarno Trulli	21	M197	Hart	V8		18	9
27/04	SAN MARINO	Imola	Ukyo Katayama	20	M197	Hart	V8		22	11
			Jarno Trulli	21	M197	Hart	V8	hydraulics on parade lap	20	ns
11/05	MONACO	Monte-Carlo	Ukyo Katayama	20	M197	Hart	V8		20	10
			Jarno Trulli	21	M197	Hart	V8	accident	18	r
25/05	SPAIN	Montmeló	Ukyo Katayama	20	M197	Hart	V8	hydraulics	20	r
			Jarno Trulli	21	M197	Hart	V8		18	15
15/06	CANADA	Montréal	Ukyo Katayama	20	M197	Hart	V8	throttle jammed/ accident	22	r
			Jarno Trulli	21	M197	Hart	V8	engine	20	r
29/06	FRANCE	Magny-Cours	Ukyo Katayama	20	M197	Hart	V8		21	11
			Tarso Marques	21	M197	Hart	V8	engine	22	r
13/07	BRITAIN	Silverstone	Ukyo Katayama	20	M197	Hart	V8	accident	18	r
			Tarso Marques	21	M197	Hart	V8		20	10
27/07	GERMANY	Hockenheim	Ukyo Katayama	20	M197	Hart	V8	out of fuel	22	r
			Tarso Marques	21	M197	Hart	V8	transmission	21	r
10/08	HUNGARY	Hungaroring	Ukyo Katayama	20	M197	Hart	V8		20	10
			Tarso Marques	21	M197	Hart	V8		22	12
24/08	BELGIUM	Spa-Francorchamps	Ukyo Katayama	20	M197	Hart	V8	engine	20	14r
			Tarso Marques	21	M197	Hart	V8	spin	22	r
07/09	ITALY	Monza	Ukyo Katayama	20	M197	Hart	V8	front wheel rim/ tyre/ accident	21	r
			Tarso Marques	21	M197	Hart	V8		22	14
21/09	AUSTRIA	A1-Ring	Ukyo Katayama	20	M197	Hart	V8		19	11
			Tarso Marques	21	M197	Hart	V8	car under weight during practice		exc
28/09	LUXEMBOURG	Nürburgring	Ukyo Katayama	20	M197	Hart	V8	accident damage	22	r
			Tarso Marques	21	M197	Hart	V8	engine	18	r
12/10	JAPAN	Suzuka	Ukyo Katayama	20	M197	Hart	V8	engine	18	r
			Tarso Marques	21	M197	Hart	V8	gearbox	19	r
26/10	EUROPE	Jerez de la Frontera	Ukyo Katayama	20	M197	Hart	V8		19	17
			Tarso Marques	21	M197	Hart	V8		20	15
1998										
08/03	AUSTRALIA	Melbourne	Shinji Nakano	22	M198	Ford Cosworth	V10	driveshaft	22	r
			Esteban Tuero	23	M198	Ford Cosworth	V10	engine	17	r
29/03	BRAZIL	Interlagos	Shinji Nakano	22	M198	Ford Cosworth	V10	spin	18	r
			Esteban Tuero	23	M198	Ford Cosworth	V10	gearbox	19	r
12/04	ARGENTINA	Buenos Aires	Shinji Nakano	22	M198	Ford Cosworth	V10		19	13
			Esteban Tuero	23	M198	Ford Cosworth	V10	accident	20	r

26/04	SAN MARINO	Imola	Shinji Nakano	22	M198	Ford Cosworth	V10	engine/ fire	21	r
			Esteban Tuero	23	M198	Ford Cosworth	V10		19	8
10/05	SPAIN	Montmeló	Shinji Nakano	22	M198	Ford Cosworth	V10		20	14
			Esteban Tuero	23	M198	Ford Cosworth	V10		19	15
24/05	MONACO	Monte-Carlo	Shinji Nakano	22	M198	Ford Cosworth	V10		19	9
			Esteban Tuero	23	M198	Ford Cosworth	V10	accident	21	r
07/06	CANADA	Montréal	Shinji Nakano	22	M198	Ford Cosworth	V10		18	7
			Esteban Tuero	23	M198	Ford Cosworth	V10	electrics	21	r
28/06	FRANCE	Magny-Cours	Shinji Nakano	22	M198	Ford Cosworth	V10	engine	21	17r
			Esteban Tuero	23	M198	Ford Cosworth	V10	gearbox	22	r
12/07	BRITAIN	Silverstone	Shinji Nakano	22	M198	Ford Cosworth	V10		19	8
			Esteban Tuero	23	M198	Ford Cosworth	V10	spin	18	r
26/07	AUSTRIA	A1-Ring	Shinji Nakano	22	M198	Ford Cosworth	V10		21	11
			Esteban Tuero	23	M198	Ford Cosworth	V10	spin	19	r
02/08	GERMANY	Hockenheim	Shinji Nakano	22	M198	Ford Cosworth	V10	gearbox	20	r
			Esteban Tuero	23	M198	Ford Cosworth	V10		21	16
16/08	HUNGARY	Hungaroring	Shinji Nakano	22	M198	Ford Cosworth	V10		19	15
			Esteban Tuero	23	M198	Ford Cosworth	V10	gearbox	21	r
30/08	BELGIUM	Spa-Francorchamps	Shinji Nakano	22	M198	Ford Cosworth	V10		21	8
			Esteban Tuero	23	M198	Ford Cosworth	V10	electrics	22	r
13/09	ITALY	Monza	Shinji Nakano	22	M198	Ford Cosworth	V10	engine/ fire	21	r
			Esteban Tuero	23	M198	Ford Cosworth	V10		22	11
27/09	LUXEMBOURG	Nürburgring	Shinji Nakano	22	M198	Ford Cosworth	V10		20	15
			Esteban Tuero	23	M198	Ford Cosworth	V10		21	nc
01/11	JAPAN	Suzuka	Shinji Nakano	22	M198	Ford Cosworth	V10	throttle	20	r
			Esteban Tuero	23	M198	Ford Cosworth	V10	accident	21	r
1999										
07/03	AUSTRALIA	Melbourne	Luca Badoer	20	M01	Ford Cosworth	V10	gearbox	21	r
			Marc Gené	21	M01	Ford Cosworth	V10	accident	22	r
11/04	BRAZIL	Interlagos	Stéphane Sarrazin	20	M01	Ford Cosworth	V10	throttle/ accident	17	r
			Marc Gené	21	M01	Ford Cosworth	V10		20	9
02/05	SAN MARINO	Imola	Luca Badoer	20	M01	Ford Cosworth	V10		22	8
			Marc Gené	21	M01	Ford Cosworth	V10		21	9
16/05	MONACO	Monte-Carlo	Luca Badoer	20	M01	Ford Cosworth	V10	gearbox	20	r
			Marc Gené	21	M01	Ford Cosworth	V10	accident	22	r
30/05	SPAIN	Montmeló	Luca Badoer	20	M01	Ford Cosworth	V10	spin	22	r
			Marc Gené	21	M01	Ford Cosworth	V10	gearbox	21	r
13/06	CANADA	Montréal	Luca Badoer	20	M01	Ford Cosworth	V10		21	10
			Marc Gené	21	M01	Ford Cosworth	V10		22	8
27/06	FRANCE	Magny-Cours	Luca Badoer	20	M01	Ford Cosworth	V10		21	10
			Marc Gené	21	M01	Ford Cosworth	V10	spin	22	r

11/07	BRITAIN	Silverstone	Luca Badoer	20	M01	Ford Cosworth	V10	gearbox	21	r
			Marc Gené	21	M01	Ford Cosworth	V10		22	15
25/07	AUSTRIA	A1-Ring	Luca Badoer	20	M01	Ford Cosworth	V10		19	13
			Marc Gené	21	M01	Ford Cosworth	V10		22	11
01/08	GERMANY	Hockenheim	Luca Badoer	20	M01	Ford Cosworth	V10		19	10
			Marc Gené	21	M01	Ford Cosworth	V10		15	9
15/08	HUNGARY	Hungaroring	Luca Badoer	20	M01	Ford Cosworth	V10		19	14
			Marc Gené	21	M01	Ford Cosworth	V10		22	17
29/08	BELGIUM	Spa-Francorchamps	Luca Badoer	20	M01	Ford Cosworth	V10	brakes/ suspension	20	r
			Marc Gené	21	M01	Ford Cosworth	V10		21	16
12/09	ITALY	Monza	Luca Badoer	20	M01	Ford Cosworth	V10	accident	19	r
			Marc Gené	21	M01	Ford Cosworth	V10	accident	20	r
26/09	EUROPE	Nürburgring	Luca Badoer	20	M01	Ford Cosworth	V10	gearbox	19	r
			Marc Gené	21	M01	Ford Cosworth	V10		20	6
17/10	MALAYSIA	Sepang	Luca Badoer	20	M01	Ford Cosworth	V10	engine overheating	21	r
			Marc Gené	21	M01	Ford Cosworth	V10		19	9
31/10	JAPAN	Suzuka	Luca Badoer	20	M01	Ford Cosworth	V10	engine	22	r
			Marc Gené	21	M01	Ford Cosworth	V10	gearbox	20	r
2000										
12/03	AUSTRALIA	Melbourne	Marc Gené	20	M02	Fondmetal	V10		18	8
			Gastón Mazzacane	21	M02	Fondmetal	V10	gearbox	22	r
26/03	BRAZIL	Interlagos	Marc Gené	20	M02	Fondmetal	V10	engine	18	r
			Gastón Mazzacane	21	M02	Fondmetal	V10		20	10
09/04	SAN MARINO	Imola	Marc Gené	20	M02	Fondmetal	V10	spin	21	r
			Gastón Mazzacane	21	M02	Fondmetal	V10		20	13
23/04	BRITAIN	Silverstone	Marc Gené	20	M02	Fondmetal	V10		21	14
			Gastón Mazzacane	21	M02	Fondmetal	V10		22	15
07/05	SPAIN	Montmeló	Marc Gené	20	M02	Fondmetal	V10		20	14
			Gastón Mazzacane	21	M02	Fondmetal	V10		21	15
21/05	EUROPE	Nürburgring	Marc Gené	20	M02	Fondmetal	V10	throttle pedal	20	r
			Gastón Mazzacane	21	M02	Fondmetal	V10		21	8
04/06	MONACO	Monte-Carlo	Marc Gené	20	M02	Fondmetal	V10	gearbox	21	r
			Gastón Mazzacane	21	M02	Fondmetal	V10	accident	22	r
18/06	CANADA	Montréal	Marc Gené	20	M02	Fondmetal	V10	spin	20	16r
			Gastón Mazzacane	21	M02	Fondmetal	V10		22	12
02/07	FRANCE	Magny-Cours	Marc Gené	20	M02	Fondmetal	V10		21	15
			Gastón Mazzacane	21	M02	Fondmetal	V10	spin	22	r
16/07	AUSTRIA	A1-Ring	Marc Gené	20	M02	Fondmetal	V10		20	8
			Gastón Mazzacane	21	M02	Fondmetal	V10		22	12
30/07	GERMANY	Hockenheim	Marc Gené	20	M02	Fondmetal	V10	engine	22	r
			Gastón Mazzacane	21	M02	Fondmetal	V10		21	11

13/08	HUNGARY	Hungaroring	Marc Gené	20	M02	Fondmetal	V10		21	15
			Gastón Mazzacane	21	M02	Fondmetal	V10	engine	22	r
27/08	BELGIUM	Spa-Francorchamps	Marc Gené	20	M02	Fondmetal	V10		21	14
			Gastón Mazzacane	21	M02	Fondmetal	V10		22	17
10/09	ITALY	Monza	Marc Gené	20	M02	Fondmetal	V10		21	9
			Gastón Mazzacane	21	M02	Fondmetal	V10		22	10
24/09	USA	Indianapolis	Marc Gené	20	M02	Fondmetal	V10		22	12
			Gastón Mazzacane	21	M02	Fondmetal	V10	engine	21	r
08/10	JAPAN	Suzuka	Marc Gené	20	M02	Fondmetal	V10	engine	21	r
			Gastón Mazzacane	21	M02	Fondmetal	V10		22	15
22/10	MALAYSIA	Sepang	Marc Gené	20	M02	Fondmetal	V10	rear wheel	21	r
			Gastón Mazzacane	21	M02	Fondmetal	V10	engine	22	13r
2001										
04/03	AUSTRALIA	Melbourne	Tarso Marques	20	PS01	European	V10	electrics	22	r
			Fernando Alonso	21	PS01	European	V10		19	12
18/03	MALAYSIA	Sepang	Tarso Marques	20	PS01	European	V10		20	14
			Fernando Alonso	21	PS01	European	V10		21	13
01/04	BRAZIL	Interlagos	Tarso Marques	20	PS01	European	V10		22	9
			Fernando Alonso	21	PS01	European	V10	throttle potentiometer	19	r
15/04	SAN MARINO	Imola	Tarso Marques	20	PS01	European	V10	engine	22	r
			Fernando Alonso	21	PS01	European	V10	accident	18	r
29/04	SPAIN	Montmeló	Tarso Marques	20	PS01	European	V10		22	16
			Fernando Alonso	21	PS01	European	V10		18	13
13/05	AUSTRIA	A1-Ring	Tarso Marques	20	PS01	European	V10	gearbox	22	r
			Fernando Alonso	21	PS01	European	V10	clutch/ gearbox	18	r
27/05	MONACO	Monte-Carlo	Tarso Marques	20	PS01	European	V10	driveshaft	22	r
			Fernando Alonso	21	PS01	European	V10	gearbox	18	r
10/06	CANADA	Montréal	Tarso Marques	20	PS01	European	V10		21	9
			Fernando Alonso	21	PS01	European	V10	driveshaft	22	r
24/06	EUROPE	Nürburgring	Tarso Marques	20	PS01	European	V10	gearbox	22	r
			Fernando Alonso	21	PS01	European	V10		21	14
01/07	FRANCE	Magny-Cours	Tarso Marques	20	PS01	European	V10		22	15
			Fernando Alonso	21	PS01	European	V10	engine	21	17r
15/07	BRITAIN	Silverstone	Tarso Marques	20	PS01	European	V10			nq
			Fernando Alonso	21	PS01	European	V10		21	16
29/07	GERMANY	Hockenheim	Tarso Marques	20	PS01	European	V10	gearbox	22	r
			Fernando Alonso	21	PS01	European	V10		21	10
19/08	HUNGARY	Hungaroring	Tarso Marques	20	PS01	European	V10	oil leak/ engine	22	r
			Fernando Alonso	21	PS01	European	V10	brakes/ spin	18	r
02/09	BELGIUM	Spa-Francorchamps	Tarso Marques	20	PS01	European	V10		22	13
			Fernando Alonso	21	PS01	European	V10	gearbox *	20	r

16/09	ITALY	Monza	Alex Yoong	20	PS01	European	V10	spin	22	r
			Fernando Alonso	21	PS01	European	V10		21	13
30/09	USA	Indianapolis	Alex Yoong	20	PS01	European	V10	gearbox	22	r
			Fernando Alonso	21	PS01	European	V10	driveshaft	17	r
14/10	JAPAN	Suzuka	Alex Yoong	20	PS01	European	V10		22	16
			Fernando Alonso	21	PS01	European	V10		18	11
* = retired after first start										
2002										
03/03	AUSTRALIA	Melbourne	Alex Yoong	22	PS02	Asiatech	V10		21	7
			Mark Webber	23	PS02	Asiatech	V10		18	5
17/03	MALAYSIA	Sepang	Alex Yoong	22	PS02	Asiatech	V10	gearbox	22	r
			Mark Webber	23	PS02	Asiatech	V10	electrics	21	r
31/03	BRAZIL	Interlagos	Alex Yoong	22	PS02	Asiatech	V10		22	13
			Mark Webber	23	PS02	Asiatech	V10		20	11
14/04	SAN MARINO	Imola	Alex Yoong	22	PS02	Asiatech	V10			nq
			Mark Webber	23	PS02	Asiatech	V10		19	11
28/04	SPAIN	Montmeló	Alex Yoong	22	PS02	Asiatech	V10	safety concern re wing failures		ew
			Mark Webber	23	PS02	Asiatech	V10	safety concern re wing failures		ew
12/05	AUSTRIA	A1-Ring	Alex Yoong	22	PS02	Asiatech	V10	engine	22	r
			Mark Webber	23	PS02	Asiatech	V10		21	12
26/05	MONACO	Monte-Carlo	Alex Yoong	22	PS02	Asiatech	V10	accident	22	r
			Mark Webber	23	PS02	Asiatech	V10		19	11
09/06	CANADA	Montréal	Alex Yoong	22	PS02	Asiatech	V10		22	14
			Mark Webber	23	PS02	Asiatech	V10		21	11
23/06	EUROPE	Nürburgring	Alex Yoong	22	PS02	Asiatech	V10	hydraulics	22	r
			Mark Webber	23	PS02	Asiatech	V10		20	15
07/07	BRITAIN	Silverstone	Alex Yoong	22	PS02	Asiatech	V10			nq
			Mark Webber	23	PS02	Asiatech	V10	clutch/ spin	20	r
21/07	FRANCE	Magny-Cours	Alex Yoong	22	PS02	Asiatech	V10		19	10
			Mark Webber	23	PS02	Asiatech	V10		18	8
28/07	GERMANY	Hockenheim	Alex Yoong	22	PS02	Asiatech	V10			nq
			Mark Webber	23	PS02	Asiatech	V10	hydraulics	21	r
18/08	HUNGARY	Hungaroring	Anthony Davidson	22	PS02	Asiatech	V10	spin	20	r
			Mark Webber	23	PS02	Asiatech	V10		19	16
01/09	BELGIUM	Spa-Francorchamps	Anthony Davidson	22	PS02	Asiatech	V10	spin	20	r
			Mark Webber	23	PS02	Asiatech	V10	gearbox	19	r
15/09	ITALY	Monza	Alex Yoong	22	PS02	Asiatech	V10		20	13
			Mark Webber	23	PS02	Asiatech	V10	electrics	19	r
29/09	USA	Indianapolis	Alex Yoong	22	PS02	Asiatech	V10	oil pump/ engine	20	r

			Mark Webber	23	PS02	Asiatech	V10	steering	18	r
13/10	JAPAN	Suzuka	Alex Yoong	22	PS02	Asiatech	V10	spin	19	r
			Mark Webber	23	PS02	Asiatech	V10		18	10
2003										
09/03	AUSTRALIA	Melbourne	Justin Wilson	18	PS03	Ford Cosworth	V10	radiator	19	r
			Jos Verstappen	19	PS03	Ford Cosworth	V10		20	11
23/03	MALAYSIA	Sepang	Justin Wilson	18	PS03	Ford Cosworth	V10	driver discomfort	19	r
			Jos Verstappen	19	PS03	Ford Cosworth	V10		18	13
06/04	BRAZIL	Interlagos	Justin Wilson	18	PS03	Ford Cosworth	V10	spin	20	r
			Jos Verstappen	19	PS03	Ford Cosworth	V10	accident	19	r
20/04	SAN MARINO	Imola	Justin Wilson	18	PS03	Ford Cosworth	V10	fuel rig	18	r
			Jos Verstappen	19	PS03	Ford Cosworth	V10	electrics	20	r
			Matteo Bobbi	39	PS03	Ford Cosworth	V10			ap
04/05	SPAIN	Montmeló	Justin Wilson	18	PS03	Ford Cosworth	V10		18	11
			Jos Verstappen	19	PS03	Ford Cosworth	V10		19	12
18/05	AUSTRIA	A1-Ring	Justin Wilson	18	PS03	Ford Cosworth	V10		18	13
			Jos Verstappen	19	PS03	Ford Cosworth	V10	launch control *	20	r
01/06	MONACO	Monte-Carlo	Justin Wilson	18	PS03	Ford Cosworth	V10	fuel feed	19	r
			Jos Verstappen	19	PS03	Ford Cosworth	V10	fuel feed	18	r
15/06	CANADA	Montréal	Justin Wilson	18	PS03	Ford Cosworth	V10	gearbox	18	r
			Jos Verstappen	19	PS03	Ford Cosworth	V10		15	9
29/06	EUROPE	Nürburgring	Justin Wilson	18	PS03	Ford Cosworth	V10		19	13
			Jos Verstappen	19	PS03	Ford Cosworth	V10		18	14
06/07	FRANCE	Magny-Cours	Justin Wilson	18	PS03	Ford Cosworth	V10		20	14
			Jos Verstappen	19	PS03	Ford Cosworth	V10		19	16
20/07	BRITAIN	Silverstone	Justin Wilson	18	PS03	Ford Cosworth	V10		18	16
			Jos Verstappen	19	PS03	Ford Cosworth	V10		19	15
03/08	GERMANY	Hockenheim	Nicolas Kiesa	18	PS03	Ford Cosworth	V10		20	12
			Jos Verstappen	19	PS03	Ford Cosworth	V10	hydraulics	19	r
			Gianmaria Bruni	39	PS03	Ford Cosworth	V10			ap
24/08	HUNGARY	Hungaroring	Nicolas Kiesa	18	PS03	Ford Cosworth	V10		20	13
			Jos Verstappen	19	PS03	Ford Cosworth	V10		18	12
			Gianmaria Bruni	39	PS03	Ford Cosworth	V10			ap
14/09	ITALY	Monza	Nicolas Kiesa	18	PS03	Ford Cosworth	V10		19	12
			Jos Verstappen	19	PS03	Ford Cosworth	V10	oil leak	17	r
			Gianmaria Bruni	39	PS03	Ford Cosworth	V10			ap
28/09	USA	Indianapolis	Nicolas Kiesa	18	PS03	Ford Cosworth	V10		20	11
			Jos Verstappen	19	PS03	Ford Cosworth	V10		19	10
			Gianmaria Bruni	39	PS03	Ford Cosworth	V10			ap
12/10	JAPAN	Suzuka	Nicolas Kiesa	18	PS03	Ford Cosworth	V10		18	16
			Jos Verstappen	19	PS03	Ford Cosworth	V10		17	15

			Gianmaria Bruni	39	PS03	Ford Cosworth	V10			ap
										* = retired after first start
2004										
07/03	AUSTRALIA	Melbourne	Gianmaria Bruni	20	PS04B	Ford Cosworth	V10		20	nc
			Zsolt Baumgartner	21	PS04B	Ford Cosworth	V10	electronics	17	r
21/03	MALAYSIA	Sepang	Gianmaria Bruni	20	PS04B	Ford Cosworth	V10		16	14
			Zsolt Baumgartner	21	PS04B	Ford Cosworth	V10		17	16
			Bas Leinders	40	PS04B	Ford Cosworth	V10			ap
04/04	BAHRAIN	Sakhir	Gianmaria Bruni	20	PS04B	Ford Cosworth	V10		17	17
			Zsolt Baumgartner	21	PS04B	Ford Cosworth	V10	engine	20	r
			Bas Leinders	40	PS04B	Ford Cosworth	V10			ap
25/04	SAN MARINO	Imola	Gianmaria Bruni	20	PS04B	Ford Cosworth	V10	brakes	17	r
			Zsolt Baumgartner	21	PS04B	Ford Cosworth	V10		18	15
			Bas Leinders	40	PS04B	Ford Cosworth	V10			ap
09/05	SPAIN	Montmeló	Gianmaria Bruni	20	PS04B	Ford Cosworth	V10	brakes/ spin	18	r
			Zsolt Baumgartner	21	PS04B	Ford Cosworth	V10	spin	20	r
			Bas Leinders	40	PS04B	Ford Cosworth	V10			ap
23/05	MONACO	Monte-Carlo	Gianmaria Bruni	20	PS04B	Ford Cosworth	V10	gearbox	20	r
			Zsolt Baumgartner	21	PS04B	Ford Cosworth	V10		19	9
			Bas Leinders	40	PS04B	Ford Cosworth	V10			ap
30/05	EUROPE	Nürburgring	Gianmaria Bruni	20	PS04B	Ford Cosworth	V10		19	14
			Zsolt Baumgartner	21	PS04B	Ford Cosworth	V10		17	15
			Bas Leinders	40	PS04B	Ford Cosworth	V10			ap
13/06	CANADA	Montréal	Gianmaria Bruni	20	PS04B	Ford Cosworth	V10	gearbox	19	r
			Zsolt Baumgartner	21	PS04B	Ford Cosworth	V10		18	10
			Bas Leinders	40	PS04B	Ford Cosworth	V10			ap
20/06	USA	Indianapolis	Gianmaria Bruni	20	PS04B	Ford Cosworth	V10	accident	18	r
			Zsolt Baumgartner	21	PS04B	Ford Cosworth	V10		19	8
			Bas Leinders	40	PS04B	Ford Cosworth	V10			ap
04/07	FRANCE	Magny-Cours	Gianmaria Bruni	20	PS04B	Ford Cosworth	V10	gearbox oil leak	19	18r
			Zsolt Baumgartner	21	PS04B	Ford Cosworth	V10	accident	20	r
			Bas Leinders	40	PS04B	Ford Cosworth	V10			ap
11/07	BRITAIN	Silverstone	Gianmaria Bruni	20	PS04B	Ford Cosworth	V10		18	16
			Zsolt Baumgartner	21	PS04B	Ford Cosworth	V10	engine	19	r
			Bas Leinders	40	PS04B	Ford Cosworth	V10			ap
25/07	GERMANY	Hockenheim	Gianmaria Bruni	20	PS04B	Ford Cosworth	V10		19	17
			Zsolt Baumgartner	21	PS04B	Ford Cosworth	V10		20	16
			Bas Leinders	40	PS04B	Ford Cosworth	V10			ap
15/08	HUNGARY	Hungaroring	Gianmaria Bruni	20	PS04B	Ford Cosworth	V10		19	14
			Zsolt Baumgartner	21	PS04B	Ford Cosworth	V10		18	15
			Bas Leinders	40	PS04B	Ford Cosworth	V10			ap

29/08	BELGIUM	Spa-Francorchamps	Gianmaria Bruni	20	PS04B	Ford Cosworth	V10	accident	17	r
			Zsolt Baumgartner	21	PS04B	Ford Cosworth	V10	accident	18	r
			Bas Leinders	40	PS04B	Ford Cosworth	V10			ap
12/09	ITALY	Monza	Gianmaria Bruni	20	PS04B	Ford Cosworth	V10	breathing problem after pit fire	18	r
			Zsolt Baumgartner	21	PS04B	Ford Cosworth	V10		19	15
			Bas Leinders	40	PS04B	Ford Cosworth	V10			ap
26/09	CHINA	Shanghai	Gianmaria Bruni	20	PS04B	Ford Cosworth	V10	front wheel lost	17	r
			Zsolt Baumgartner	21	PS04B	Ford Cosworth	V10		19	16
			Bas Leinders	40	PS04B	Ford Cosworth	V10			ap
10/10	JAPAN	Suzuka	Gianmaria Bruni	20	PS04B	Ford Cosworth	V10		18	16
			Zsolt Baumgartner	21	PS04B	Ford Cosworth	V10	accident	20	r
			Bas Leinders	40	PS04B	Ford Cosworth	V10			ap
24/10	BRAZIL	Interlagos	Gianmaria Bruni	20	PS04B	Ford Cosworth	V10		19	17
			Zsolt Baumgartner	21	PS04B	Ford Cosworth	V10		20	16
			Bas Leinders	40	PS04B	Ford Cosworth	V10			ap
2005										
06/03	AUSTRALIA	Melbourne	Patrick Friesacher	20	PS04B	Cosworth	V10		16	17
			Christijan Albers	21	PS04B	Cosworth	V10	gearbox	17	r
20/03	MALAYSIA	Sepang	Patrick Friesacher	20	PS04B	Cosworth	V10	spin	20	r
			Christijan Albers	21	PS04B	Cosworth	V10		19	13
03/04	BAHRAIN	Sakhir	Patrick Friesacher	20	PS04B	Cosworth	V10		19	12
			Christijan Albers	21	PS04B	Cosworth	V10		18	13
24/04	SAN MARINO	Imola	Patrick Friesacher	20	PS05	Cosworth	V10	gearbox shaft	19	r
			Christijan Albers	21	PS05	Cosworth	V10	gearbox fluid leak	20	r
08/05	SPAIN	Montmeló	Patrick Friesacher	20	PS05	Cosworth	V10	spin	15	r
			Christijan Albers	21	PS05	Cosworth	V10	gearbox	14	r
22/05	MONACO	Monte-Carlo	Patrick Friesacher	20	PS05	Cosworth	V10	accident	13	r
			Christijan Albers	21	PS05	Cosworth	V10		14	14
29/05	EUROPE	Nürburgring	Patrick Friesacher	20	PS05	Cosworth	V10		18	18
			Christijan Albers	21	PS05	Cosworth	V10		20	17
12/06	CANADA	Montréal	Patrick Friesacher	20	PS05	Cosworth	V10	hydraulics	19	r
			Christijan Albers	21	PS05	Cosworth	V10		15	11
19/06	USA	Indianapolis	Patrick Friesacher	20	PS05	Cosworth	V10		20	6
			Christijan Albers	21	PS05	Cosworth	V10		18	5
03/07	FRANCE	Magny-Cours	Patrick Friesacher	20	PS05	Cosworth	V10	tyre	18	r
			Christijan Albers	21	PS05	Cosworth	V10	tyre	20	r
10/07	BRITAIN	Silverstone	Patrick Friesacher	20	PS05	Cosworth	V10		19	19
			Christijan Albers	21	PS05	Cosworth	V10		18	18
24/07	GERMANY	Hockenheim	Robert Doornbos	20	PS05	Cosworth	V10		17	18
			Christijan Albers	21	PS05	Cosworth	V10		16	13

31/07	HUNGARY	Hungaroring	Robert Doornbos	20	PS05	Cosworth	V10	hydraulics	19	r
			Christijan Albers	21	PS05	Cosworth	V10	hydraulics	17	r
			Chanoch Nissany	40	PS05	Cosworth	V10			ap
21/08	TURKEY	Istanbul	Robert Doornbos	20	PS05	Cosworth	V10		17	13
			Christijan Albers	21	PS05	Cosworth	V10	withdrawn	15	r
			Enrico Toccacelo	40	PS05	Cosworth	V10			ap
04/09	ITALY	Monza	Robert Doornbos	20	PS05	Cosworth	V10		18	18
			Christijan Albers	21	PS05	Cosworth	V10		20	19
			Enrico Toccacelo	40	PS05	Cosworth	V10			ap
11/09	BELGIUM	Spa-Francorchamps	Robert Doornbos	20	PS05	Cosworth	V10		17	13
			Christijan Albers	21	PS05	Cosworth	V10		18	12
			Enrico Toccacelo	40	PS05	Cosworth	V10			ap
25/09	BRAZIL	Interlagos	Robert Doornbos	20	PS05	Cosworth	V10	oil pipe	18	r
			Christijan Albers	21	PS05	Cosworth	V10		16	14
09/10	JAPAN	Suzuka	Robert Doornbos	20	PS05	Cosworth	V10		15	14
			Christijan Albers	21	PS05	Cosworth	V10		13	16
16/10	CHINA	Shanghai	Robert Doornbos	20	PS05	Cosworth	V10		20	14
			Christijan Albers	21	PS05	Cosworth	V10		18	16

YEAR	TOTAL CONSTRUCTORS	MINARDI PLACING	POINTS
1985	17		0
1986	14		0
1987	16		0
1988	18	10th	1
1989	20	10th equal	6
1990	19		0
1991	18	7th	6
1992	16	11th equal	1
1993	13	8th	7
1994	14	10th	5
1995	13	10th	1
1996	11		0
1997	12		0
1998	11		0
1999	11	9th equal	1
2000	11		0
2001	11		0
2002	11	9th equal	2
2003	10		0
2004	10	10th	1
2005	10	10th	7

More from Veloce Publishing

BRM V16

How Britain's auto makers built a Grand Prix car to beat the world

Karl Ludvigsen

Hardback • 25x25cm • £17.99 • 96 pages.
• 160 colour & b&w photos/illustrations
• ISBN: 978-1-845840-37-2 • UPC: 6-36847-04037-6

Few racing cars of any kind have a more exotic and exciting reputation among enthusiasts than the first BRM, a 16-cylinder wonder machine that was a bright beacon of promise in Britain's drab post-war years. Packed with photos from the author's collection, this is the story of a bold but ultimately misguided venture that delivered too much, too late.

BRM – A mechanic's tale

Dick Salmon

Hardback • 25x25cm • £39.99 • 224 pages
• 275 colour & b&w photos
• ISBN 978-184584082-2 • UPC: 6-36847-04028-4

The inside story told by a man who was both a devoted fan and loyal team member of British Racing Motors from the 1950s. Graham Hill drove the BRM to victory to win both the Drivers' World Championship and the Constructors' Championship for the BRM team, a considerable contribution to British motor racing history.

* prices subject to change. p+p extra. for more details visit www.veloce.co.uk or email info@veloce.co.uk.

More from Veloce Publishing

Porsche Racing Cars 1953 to 1975

Brian Long

Hardback • 250x250mm • £45 • 272 pages
• c.600 colour & mono photographs
• ISBN: 978-1-904788-44-7 • UPC: 6-36847-00344-9

Follows Porsche's year-by-year progress in top flight racing, and looks in detail at the pure competition cars that brought the German marque such immense success and worldwide acclaim on the tracks. This particular volume starts with the story of the giant-killing 550 Spyders of 1953 vintage, and takes the reader through all the susbsequent racing models.

The Bahamas Speed Weeks

Terry O'Neil

Hardback • 25x25cm • £55.00 • 368 pages
• 456 colour & b&w photos
• ISBN: 978-1-84584-018-1 • UPC: 6-36847-04018-5

From the mid-1950s, the Bahamian island of New Providence hosted Speed Weeks for 13 years. Seen by many as the 'Golden Age' of motor racing, internationally acclaimed drivers mixed with amateur racers who came to enjoy the sun, parties and racing. This book chronicles the ups and downs of these often glamourous, always exciting, events.

* prices subject to change. p+p extra. for more details visit www.veloce.co.uk or email info@veloce.co.uk.

1½-litre Grand Prix Racing 1961-65

Mark Whitelock

Hardback • 25x25cm • £39.99 • 336 pages • 200+b&w illustrations • ISBN: 978-1-84584-016-7 • UPC: 6-36847-04016-1

The story of a Grand Prix formula that no British constructor wanted but which they came to almost totally dominate. It saw the career of Stirling Moss come to a premature end, and, in his absence, the rise to prominence of a new breed of British driver in Jim Clark, Graham Hill and John Surtees.

Motor Racing
– Reflections of a Lost Era

Anthony Carter

Hardback • 25x25cm • £39.99 • 208 pages • 300 colour & b&w illustrations • ISBN: 978-1-904788-10-2 • UPC: 6-36847-00310-4

A defining era in motorsport documented in words and intimate photographs, both black & white and colour, from the mid-1950s through the 1960s, when motor racing was still accessible to all, to the 1970s when overt sponsorship and television changed the sport forever.

Index

LOST BOYS